The Lucifer Connection

93 Visualization very popular in Charismatics & pentacostals
96 "   " in the medical profession

The Lucifer Connection

by Joseph Carr

HUNTINGTON HOUSE, INC.

Huntington House, Inc.
Lafayette, Louisiana

Library of Congress Card Number 87-81608
ISBN Number 0-910311-42-0

Printed in the United States of America
Typographical and cover designs by Publications Technologies

About this Book

Two different readers were in mind when this book was planned. The first is the Christian reader who needs information about (and awareness of) the New Age Movement and the doctrine of reincarnation. For this reason, the book was published by a Christian publisher and is sold primarily through Christian ministries, and in Christian bookstores.

The second reader is the non-Christian who puts his or her hope for eternity in a false religious system. Few of those people will see this book unless you take action. If you know a person who believes in, or dabbles with, any of the occultic things in this book, or who was influenced by Shirley MacLaine's book, and ABC-TV miniseries *Out On A Limb*, then please buy them a gift copy of this book.

Contents

Introduction

Arlington County, Virginia, and Washington, D.C. together form the 10-mile square allowed by the U.S. Constitution for the nation's capital. Although long ago ceded back to Virginia, Arlington was Washington's western bedroom community during my childhood years.

My old neighborhood (Madison Manor/Dominion Hills) is a couple dozen or so blocks of two-story colonials and single-story ramblers built right after World War II to house the flood of families started by returning veterans.

The neighborhood was bounded on the north by Four Mile Run Creek (now Interstate 66) and on the south by Wilson Boulevard. At the southwest corner of the neighborhood, across Wilson Boulevard from the big water tower, was an estate that local gossip claimed was once the home of actress Audrey Meadows. A block or two down Wilson was the Kern Estate.

Oddly, the ideas for two of my Christian books came from famous persons who lived in or very near the old neighborhood. *The Twisted Cross* (Huntington House) was inspired in part by American neo-Nazi George Lincoln Rockwell. Although he started his irrational career in another neighborhood on the other side of the county, he ended up in Dominion Hills.

When author Alex Haley (of *Roots* fame) interviewed Rockwell, it was probably at the Kern Estate, which the Nazis rented. One day in 1967, George Lincoln Rockwell went to do his own laundry at the coin-operated laundramat in the Dominion Hills Shopping Center less than a block from his headquarters. As the Nazi leader turned to exit his car on the driver's side, two shots from an 1896 Mauser "Broomhandle" pistol rang out and Rockwell fell dead onto the parking lot blacktop.

It turned out later that Rockwell was murdered by one of his own "storm troopers" who had hidden on the roof behind the laundramat sign. Even today, more than 20 years later, local Nazis occasionally stencil paint a foot-high swastika on the spot where Rockwell died. Although the shopping center management routinely paints out the swastikas, they always reappear within a few weeks.

The other neighborhood personality is actress Shirley Maclaine. Local gossip also told us that she grew up in that neighborhood and graduated from Washington-Lee High School a mile or so away. I know several W-L alumni who followed Shirley Maclaine's career with keen interest, even though she went through the place a decade earlier than us. Although I no longer have favorite actors or actresses, it is still easy to induce me to watch a Shirley MacLaine movie ... I suppose I am still a fan.

Recently, Shirley MacLaine has become a leading New Age advocate. In that role, she was an inspiration for this present book. Maclaine's books, *Out On A Limb* and *Dancing In The Light*, form the statement of her spiritual oddysey ...and have influenced millions of readers. On January 18-19, 1987 ABC-TV aired a heavily publicized five-hour miniseries based on *Out On A Limb*. With that telecast, many millions more were exposed to seemingly congenial New Age spiritual teachings that are eternally fatal.

Television is such an influential medium that scores of millions of people who would otherwise not pay any attention at all to the alluring blandishments of the New Age are now wondering if perhaps there is something to these "new" ideas.

Because of Shirley MacLaine's widespread influence, the collective influence of other New Agers and the ultimate importance of the questions they raise, I have decided to write this book. My task is to counter some of the claims of the New Age, especially the doctrine of reincarnation and the Law of Karma.

Joseph J. Carr
Arlington, Virginia

A New Age?

... Or an Old Lie?

The New Age Movement is the fastest growing, most significant challenge to the Church today. It looms larger than Secular Humanism because it provides something that Humanism lacks: while retaining Humanism's insistence that man is the measure of all things, it also *awakens and nurtures a fundamental religious impulse.* It is widespread, worldwide, powerful, seductively alluring and openly Luciferic.

Most New Agers profess a Western variant of Hinduism and other Eastern religions. New Age mysticism is rapidly becoming the cozy religion of the young, upwardly mobile urban professionals ("Yuppies").

The New Age Movement offers them a mystical religion that draws heavily on Eastern religions, the Western Esoteric Tradition (old-fashioned occultism) and 19th-century evolution science. The New Age claims that all religions are equally valid and all are merely different paths back to God. Thus, it is congenial to both the eclectic sophisticates and simpler folk for whom churchianity has somehow failed.

A key New Age doctrine is that humans are divine, i.e., we are gods. This heretical idea is now even being taught by once-orthodox Christian leaders, including a few radio-TV evangelists. Clearly, the New Age Movement has deeply infiltrated the Church. According to New Age teaching, our divinity is suppressed in the muck of physical reality. This divinity must be rediscovered through the Quest and is the underlying purpose behind evolution. The awakening of our divinity awareness is called "self-realization." The variant taught by Christian heretics is a little different but merely says in different words the same thing that Lucifer said to Eve (Genesis 3).

Another New Age heresy (that also infests the Church) is the idea that we can affect physical reality by our thoughts and words. Proponents of this view claim that we can take psychic dominion over the earth and all of the forces of nature. Although some proponents fail to inform us how that mammoth achievement is possible, others are not so bashful: we become manifest sons of God, hence gods ourselves.

Dare we say it? We become fully self-realized. Their teaching is not that God answers prayers and works miracles (a concept that all Christians accept) but, rather, that our words themselves have a hidden power that anyone with the right key can tap.

Whether taught by a New Ager or a Christian pastor, these doctrines are always wrong ... and ultimately deadly.

Dave Hunt and T.A. McMahon remind us in their book *The Seduction of Christianity*[1] that the proper technical names for these doctrines are "shamanism" and "sorcery." When Christians teach these doctrines to their flock, they are in essence poisoning the Communion cup.

The New Age Movement is no mere cult: it is worldwide and consists of many cults, many different groups, several non-Christian religions and many different people who share certain metaphysical ideas and experiences. The movement has spiritual, cultural and political agendas that are openly anti-Christian, mystical and Luciferic.

Some Christians believe that the New Age Movement is the movement predicted in scripture.[2] That claim may be true but I fear that the Church will focus on such romantic aspects of the movement and lose sight of a more important issue. Namely, the New Age Movement is both alluring to spiritually minded people and eternally fatal to those who drink too long from its poisoned well.

Acceptance of the New Age theology leads one to damnation. Because of this fact, the proper perspective for the Church is to view the New Age Movement as a compelling evangelistic opportunity, a fertile missions field and a challenge to rise to our responsibilities under the Great Commission.

Many New Age doctrines grew out of the "Western Esoteric Tradition" which has existed as an occultic underground in the West for more than 1,500 years. These ideas were developed further, married to Hindu and Buddhist ideas and then cast in a pseudo-scientific mold during the Occult Revival of the late 19th century.

The principal agents in this effort were Madame Helena Petrovna Blavatsky (called "HPB" by her followers) and her fellow Theosophists. It is not unreasonable to call theosophy a New Age brick in the western wall of Mystery Babylon, for theosophy forms the basis for most New Age groups. If you examine the doctrines and world views of those groups, especially those of a more outwardly religious pursuasion, then you will find more than a few of the elements of theosophical doctrine.

I once attended a day of lectures at a New Age retreat center near Baltimore, Maryland. One speaker summed his points up by explaining what was meant by the coming "New Age" and then enthusiastically concluded with a statement that should chill Bible-believing Christians: *"... it all started in Babylon, folks!"*

The New Age Movement is a descendent of the Babylonian Mystery Religion. Indeed, it rapidly becomes apparent that there is nothing new in the New Age Movement, it is the same old harlot, Mystery Babylon. What the New Age Movement has done is given her some fresh make-up and a new dress. Madame Blavatsky was the seamstress who cut the pattern for the harlot's new dress.

Blavatsky's theosophy is a uniquely Western treatment of the Eastern religious doctrines derived ultimately from the ancient mystery religions. Those same ideas filtered from ancient Babylon to the East (especially India) and to the West (through Persian Zoroasterism and Manicheanism) into Europe. The ancient heresy became the gnostic Cathar religion of Europe (among others) but then went underground for centuries because of a hostile Church.

The Eastern and Western threads of this same tradition, modified by time and circumstance, met in theosophy during the Occult Revival. It is thus not surprising to find theosophical groups leading the way to the reappearance of "the Christ" in the form of a demon named Lord Maitreya (see *Hidden Dangers of the Rainbow,* by Constance Cumbey).

Cumbey wrote that this movement meets the biblical tests for the antichrist of prophecy. Regardless of whether you agree with Constance Cumbey, it is essential that you see the historical, doctrinal and philosophical basis of the movement: *souls are at stake.*

The rawest and most gruesome expression of theosophical ideas was the crimes committed by the Nazi SS during the Holocaust.[3] Adolf Hitler's "Final Solution to the Jewish problem" was derived directly from his theosophical (metaphysical) beliefs. When the men of the SS slaughtered innocent Jews in the death camps, they were merely acting on logical conclusions drawn from the teachings of theosophy: the Law of Karma, reincarnation, the doctrine of races and so forth. Those very ideas, which propelled SS troopers to unparalleled barbarity, are at the very heart and core of the New Age Movement!

No one would claim that Shirley MacLaine and other New Agers are Nazi storm troopers. But they should be aware that the very same doctrines that they hold so dear are at the base of Naziism. The New Age Movement and Naziism are merely different branches on the same theosophical tree and it is a tree that is rotten to the core ... even though apparently healthy on the outside.

Is It A Conspiracy?

Some Christian leaders claim that the New Age Movement is a worldwide conspiracy. Others claim that the movement is totally unorganized, i.e. that it is merely a state of mind. Still others claim that the movement doesn't even exist (a position that is now so absurd as to not require comment). Some people sneer that Constance Cumbey, Dave Hunt and the others draw too much from the old discredited "Illuminati" theories of world conspiracy. We can dispose of that charge by pointing out that Cumbey and Hunt publically ridicule such theories. Only a casual, uncritical reading of their works yields such a viewpoint.

The second point against the most severe critics of Cumbey and Hunt is their almost universal use of the argument *ad hominem*. The critics have a knee-jerk reaction against all conspiracy theories, against any attack of their own possibly heretic views and anyone who would rock their comfortable boat. To those people, Cumbey is just a wild, wierd, looney lady with a strange theory.

Dave Hunt? After his book *The Seduction of Christianity* became a bestseller, they can't even give Hunt the benefit of honorable doubt. What the critics fail to do, however, is examine the claims of Cumbey and Hunt to see if they are correct. Constance Cumbey and Dave Hunt have no magical sources of information available to them alone. Both writers did substantial research and left both text references and footnotes that allow any scholar — or lay person with a brain and a little energy — to follow the same trails to see if they, indeed, lead where the writers claim. The proper response to the claims of Cumbey and Hunt is deep research, dialogue and open debate, *to see whether they are right.*

As to whether it is a conspiracy, we must note that the movement itself uses the word "conspiracy." One of the most blatant public statements of New Age plans and goals is Marylin Ferguson's *The Aquarian Conspiracy.*[4] It is demonstrable that the New Age Movement is interconnected through the phenomena of networking. The movement itself boasts of its widespread network of networks, many of which have interlocking memberships and leadership.

By using the correct code words and acceptance of common ideas, the network gains immense flexibility, near invulnerability and it functions almost like a living organism. Damage to the network, such as the Jim Jones "People's Temple" murder/suicide fiasco, can be easily repaired by disowning the embarrassing group. Before Jones' bad press, they were listed in New Age directories as a "Christian socialist New Age community;" afterwards they were quickly labelled "Christian fundamentalist."

When a knot in the network becomes unravelled,

all the movement needs to do is excise the offending portion and join the loose ends together. If extensive networking demonstrates conspiracy, then the New Age Movement is a self-admitted conspiracy.

A major problem for those who automatically reject conspiracy theories is their inability to see a hard organizational structure. Unfortunately, as mere humans, we tend to see things in human terms. When confronted with something like the New Age Movement, we fail to remember that it is Luciferian — and if Lucifer is in charge, then the movement doesn't need either a headquarters building with an address that the post office can find or a set of registered corporate bylaws.

Lucifer can operate on the spiritual level to influence and guide the conspiracy without there being a headquarters on earth or a wicked group of human conspirators at the head. A classical conspiracy has a head that can be cut off, thereby neutralizing the organization. But a collective of networks does not suffer that liability. Thus, New Age organization — or lack of it — is a diabolically clever security measure that ensures the longevity of the movement.

The evidence for a worldwide conspiracy, a loose confederation of mystics who think and act alike, is compelling and strong. Although I cannot see a classical "Illuminati" type of organization and probably nonesuch exists, there is definitely a Luciferian spiritual conspiracy afoot ... and hopefully before too long we will know what New Agers mean when they refer to "The Plan."

At present, some New Age leaders are hoping to change the name of the movement. A leading New Age teacher told me two years ago that the term had outlived its usefulness. Given that the conversation was on the effects of Cumbey's first book, I suspect that the effort to change the name (hence the identity) of the movement was, at least in part, due to *Hidden Dangers of the Rainbow*. I suspect that at least part of the New Age Movement will submerge underground in the near future, only to re-emerge a short time later in the guise of something else pretending to be sacred.

Born Again and Again?

Reincarnation and the Law of Karma

A new religious movement is taking over and transforming our society. Actress Shirley Maclaine is now one of its most prominent followers and most articulate popular spokesman. It is called the New Age Movement and it can claim more than 60 million followers in the United States alone (many millions more follow the movement worldwide). It has been called the emerging Yuppie religion. Shirley MacLaine puts forth the story of her conversion to the New Age in her book *Out On A Limb*[1] and follows up with a more detailed treatment of her belief in reincarnation in *Dancing In The Light*.[2]

There are three streams in the modern New Age Movement: Eastern religions, the Western Esoteric Tradition and Darwinian evolution theory. The Eastern religions at the base of the New Age are Zen, Buddhism and especially Hinduism. The Western Esoteric Tradition is occultism as expressed in gnosticism, Rosicrucianism, Freemasonry and other movements in European culture over the centuries.

The evolution theories of Charles Darwin are congenial to the New Age Movement. There is such startling similarity between ancient variants of New Age thinking and evolution theory that one can but wonder if the popular view of Darwin represents the real Darwin. It would be interesting to research his life to determine if there are traces of Eastern religions or Western occultism present.

According to New Age thinking, man is evolving from non-human and non-animal origins towards a superhuman being — and eventually godhood. By following New Age disciplines man can, according to this theory, hurry his ascent up the evolutionary ladder to godhood. It appears that only the end point of man differs between New Age and Darwinian theory.

Perhaps the most famous proponent of New Age theories, especially its evolution aspects, was Adolf Hitler. Even some New Agers admit that Hitler was a brother who went bad. I detail Hitler's occultic religion in my book *The Twisted Cross*.[3] Hitler's murder of the Jewish people came directly from those occultic beliefs, the very same beliefs that are taught today in the New Age Movement!

The most hideous aspect of the Holocaust, during which 6 million Jews were killed, was that it was merely a racial cleansing action. Like other New Agers, the Nazis believed that humankind would evolve through a series of seven "Root Races" of which the misnamed "Aryan" man (white northern Europeans) was the fifth.[4] They believed that Aryan man was going to make an evolutionary leap to the sixth Root Race, called *Ubermensche* (superman). Today's New Agers call the same being *Homo Noeticus* and still await the coming global leap of consciousness. Remnants of earlier Root Races, mostly the Jews, were said to be guilty of trying to prevent the leap to Superman by tainting racial blood lines. Thus, the SS man salved his conscience as he killed innocent Jews and gypsies by thinking that he was involved in race cleansing — something like vermin control (evolution is a very powerful theory!).

The SS man also took comfort in believing that he was ultimately helping those Jews he killed! They believed in reincarnation and the Law of Karma, so they felt they helped the Jews work off some "bad racial karma" through suffering a violent death. Thus, that Jewish soul could reincarnate into a higher — perhaps Aryan — body next time around.

Reincarnation and the Law of Karma was a principal Nazi doctrine and is now a principal New Age doctrine. In fact, the main teachings that make a group "New Age" are the twin doctrines of Reincarnation and the Law of Karma. Although there are exceptions, a group is not fully New Age unless it accepts those two watershed Hindu doctrines. The doctrines of reincarnation and karma cannot be separated either from each other or from the New Age Movement. If any single religious doctrine glues the New Age together it is this: it forms the linchpin of the entire movement.

Reincarnation is the doctrine that holds that the soul is immortal and spends its time in eternity being born into physical bodies, living on Earth and then dying to return to the spirit realm for a period of rest. During the rest period, the soul undergoes recuperation and reflection on the experiences and lessons learned during previous lifetimes on Earth. The word "incarnation" implies "in the flesh" or "in the physical body" so reincarnation doctrine implies that the soul repeatedly enters physical bodies on earth.

The doctrine of reincarnation came into our modern Western culture via two routes: Eastern religions (such as Hinduism and Buddhism) and the Western Esoteric Tradition. The theosophy movement in the 19th century synthesized a modified system that blended those two traditions with a crude understanding of evolution science. From those beginnings sprang both the New Age Movement ... and Naziism.

Modern reincarnation doctrine is related to the *metempsychosis* (change of souls) doctrine of the Hellenic Greeks and the Hindu doctrine of Transmigration of Souls. In the Hindu version, a soul may reincarnate into the body of either an animal or a human. Whether one goes up or down the order of Creation depends upon one's actions in the past life. Western reincarnation reflects Western values, however, so in the Western view souls only reincarnate into human bodies.

The Law of Karma inevitably tags along with reincarnation. Karma has been called the "Law of the Universe without a Lawgiver;" it is also called "The Law of Cause and Effect" by theosophists. The Law of Karma maintains that each soul earns its present condition on this earth through its actions in past lives. Karma operates automatically and mercilessly keeping a kind of cosmic balance sheet of good deeds balanced by bad deeds. In the narrow calculus of Karma, good deeds (variously defined) and suffering are needed to balance the bad deeds of past lifetimes. If a person commits an evil deed in this lifetime, then he or she will be reincarnated into a lower state in the next lifetime (possibly nonhuman).

Reincarnationists insist that justice is the essence of the Law of Karma. After all, they insist, a soul reaps only what it sows. Ultimately, when the "karmic debt" is finally paid, the soul rejoins the Source (also called "God" and "Cosmic Consciousness") and no longer needs to reincarnate. The journey has supposedly taken as little as 43 years and as long as 2 million years.

History

The doctrine of reincarnation has been the fond hope of mankind for more than 2,000 years. It appeared among the Hindus sometime prior to 300 B.C. but it is uncertain how early it was known. Some supporters of the doctrine claim that Buddha taught reincarnation around 500 B.C. It is certain the traces of the doctrine are known as early as Buddha and some speculation is permissible for a date of 700 B.C.

Western reincarnationists sometimes attempt to force a date much earlier than what is provable, however. Buddhism, which is a religion that evolved from Hinduism, also taught reincarnation from very early in its history, even though it is not known for sure whether Gautama Buddha himself taught it.

When reincarnation appeared among the Greeks (as Metempsychosis), it was taught in the ancient Mystery Schools; Socrates (fourth century B.C.) called reincarnation "... that ancient doctrine."

Under the Roman Empire, reincarnation doctrine spread throughout the Mediterranean world. It was taught by the Stoics and Neo-Platonists in the Greco-Roman world and by the Essenes in the Jewish world. As Western Europe passed through the Dark Ages into the Middle Ages, the torch of reincarnation passed to the Hermetic Schools, the Cathari and other gnostics; the Knights Templar were said to harbor reincarnationist doctrines, contrary to the doctrine of their parent Roman Catholic Church.

During the Renaissance, the Reformation and the Ages of Reason and Enlightenment, Western interest in reincarnation was at a low point. Although its popularity waned in the West, reincarnation remained an underground thread in our culture. When Europeans started traveling to the East in great numbers during the 17th and 18th centuries, they returned with increased interest in the religions of those nations.

The root of modern Western reincarnation doctrine is found in the 19th century. Three threads of mystical philosophy are found in the last century:

• The rise of American Transcendentalism (Thoreau, Emerson and others),

• The formation of the Theosophical Society by H.P. Blavatsky and others and

• The arrival of Hindu missionaries in the West (Ramakrishna Mission and Swami Vivekananda) during and after the Parliament of World Religions (1893).

Today, reincarnation is so deeply rooted in American culture that studies show as many as 40 percent of us either believe in reincarnation or at least admit its possibility. At a recent world Hindu meeting, a leader proclaimed that their mission to the West has been successful and that "Christianity is on the decrease."

Is Reincarnation Christian?

Reincarnationists insist that belief in multiple lifetimes is compatible with Christian doctrine. They claim that either:

• The Bible now implicitly teaches reincarnation or

• The Bible once explicitly taught reincarnation but was altered by the church. People who believe that scripture teaches reincarnation have a few favorite passages but must torture meanings to "prove" their point. Reincarnationists who teach that the church expunged reincarnation from the Bible like to point to these same scripture verses as evidence that the evil deed was not thorough and those verses represent residual reincarnationist doctrine.

Several questions and statements about reincarnation present themselves. First, of course, is why would the church want to expunge any given doctrine? From a purely functional point of view, what did it matter to the church fathers whether they preached reincarnation or resurrection? There is no reason to favor one over the other, *unless one is true and the other is false.*

The suppressed doctrine theory maintains that early church fathers scrapped manuscripts of the Bible that contain reincarnationist writings. There was also supposedly an early church council that intentionally deleted reincarnation from its creed. Some reincarnationists claim that editions of the "true" Bible (with reincarnation included) are on deposit in the Vatican library, where they are jealously guarded by a priesthood that does not want us to know the truth. There are even former priests who claim to have seen the manuscripts, although no copies are ever smuggled out to a waiting world.

There are more than a few problems with the claims of "Christian" reincarnationists. Regarding the "altered Bible" thesis, one has to wonder how a church, especially one that was disorganized before the fourth century A.D. and factionalized afterwards, could manage such a feat. The Greco-Roman world was flooded with copies of both Old and New Testament scriptures, so much so that suppressing a valid doctrine would be very difficult — and probably impossible.

An "altered Bible" theory dismisses the Christian claim that God protected the Bible and its translations over the centuries. What an inept god the reincarnationist worships! He is capable of creating the universe (although some New Age teachers claim that His incompetence is proved by the Creation, which they regard as a mistake) but is powerless to prevent

some silly pope from obliterating the doctrine of reincarnation from the earthly records of His effort. Such
assertions stand precariously at the edge of a logical
chasm too broad for the healthy mind to leap!

The record of proof regarding the supposed secret
church councils similarly requires an act of immense
misplaced faith. No record, no hint, no eyewitness account of such a council is presented — only the assertion that it did, indeed, occur; some people claim that
it was the Council of Nicea.[5]

The shroud of secrecy surrounding the council is
cited as evidence that no evidence is possible. After
all, if the proceedings were secret, then one would not
expect to find proof of its existence. A superficial examination makes such a claim seem attractive but it
soon falls of its own weight. In the first instance, no
church-wide council can remain totally secret for
long; especially a council that is dealing with a basic
doctrinal tenet that appears in thousands of scripture
manuscripts.

There are always either dissenters who spread the
tale or the indiscrete whose carelessness lets word go
abroad. In the second instance, if such a council were
so secret that it left no discernible record, then how
can they be so sure that it actually took place?

There are certain events in church history that
might be erroneously construed as suppression of reincarnation doctrine. The church did, in fact, select
certain manuscripts for inclusion in the Canon of
Scripture. Selection of some manuscripts implies rejection of others. The documents that were rejected
included both non-canonical Christian texts (which
were doctrinally acceptable works but failed the tests
of canonicity) and also the works of gnosticism and
other competing religions. Some of the latter documents did teach reincarnation but they could not be

regarded as "removed" from the Bible because they were never in it in the first place!

The above argument also applies to the "Vatican Library Bibles" that allegedly teach reincarnation and the Law of Karma. It is likely that an institution as old as the Roman Catholic Church and its Vatican would have collected a large number of ancient manuscripts both from Christian and non-Christian sources. Those manuscripts probably exist, but were not "Bible" manuscripts, rather were of gnostic origin.

You can go to almost any bookstore and certainly any New Age bookstore and obtain some of these ancient manuscripts reprinted in modern form: *The Lost Books of the Bible*,[6] *The Book of Enoch*,[7] *The Lost Books of Adam and Eve* and various pseudoepigraphic works, many of which are contained in the scholarly work *The Nag Hammadi Library*[8] (and discussed in Elaine Pagels' *The Gnostic Gospels*[9]). Again, those books were not removed from the Bible at all ... they were rejected as scripture by the Church in the fourth century.

There are also claims among New Agers that Jesus himself taught reincarnation and other secret doctrines. They sometimes cite Matthew 13:10-13 as evidence:

> *"And the disciples came and said to Him, 'why do you speak to them in parables?' And He answered and said to them, 'to you it has been granted to know the mysteries of the kingdom of Heaven but to them it has not been granted. For whoever has, to him shall more be given and he shall have an abundance; but whoever does not have, even what he has shall be taken away from him. Therefore I speak to them in parables; hearing they do not hear, nor do they understand'* " [NASB].

This passage is alleged to be Jesus telling the disciples that they are privy to a secret doctrine that is not available to the general public; an idea that has been popular with initiation cults for millenia. Reincarnationists who tout the Matthew passage tend to ignore John 18:20, which says:

> *"Jesus answered him, 'I have spoken openly to the world; I always taught in Synagogues and in the Temple, where all the Jews come together; and I spoke nothing in secret' "* [NASB] *(emphasis added).*

One reincarnationist whom I challenged with John 18:20 retorted that the verse was Jesus' response during his trial before the priests and he lied to save his life. The fallacy inherent in this comment is that a lying Jesus could not be trusted in any event, so why assume that his alleged teaching on reincarnation is any more truthful? It is more reasonable to assume that he told the truth on both occasions but reincarnationists err in their interpretation of Matthew 13:10-13.

There are certain manuscripts that claim to be genuine gospel documents, yet claim that Jesus taught a secret doctrine. Dr. Morton Smith, writing in *The Secret Gospel*,[10] claims to have found such an edition of the Gospel of Mark in a monastery near Jerusalem. The argument for its authenticity is weakened by the admission that it is a late manuscript copy, not an original. The so-called "secret teachings" do not appear in any of the earlier manuscripts, some of which are 1,000 years nearer the time of Mark than the monastery find.

It is certain that neither Jesus nor the church fathers taught reincarnation doctrine in any form. In fact, the church fathers actively opposed the gnostic teaching of reincarnation. Irenaeus of Lyon opposed the doctrine in his work *Against Heresies*. Theosophist G.R.S. Mead (1863-1933), himself a believer in reincarnation, wrote against the notion that the early Church taught reincarnation. His article titled "The

Reincarnationists of Early Christendom" appeared in the April 1914 edition of *The Quest*[11], a theosophical magazine:

"In popular expositions of the reincarnation theory the claim is frequently met with that some of the Church Fathers taught the doctrine. This, however, is an error, owing chiefly to the looseness of thinking that uncritically equates the general notion of the preexistence of the soul with the special theory of transcorporation in the sense of reincarnation in a series of bodies on earth. It is true that some of the Fathers valiantly defended the doctrine of preexistence; but I have yet found not a single patristic passage that favours the reincarnation theory and doubt very much that any is to be found. Not only so but Fathers who are quoted in popular books as believers in reincarnation, are found, when systematically interrogated, to reject transcorporation in the sense of reincarnation utterly."

Mead goes on further in the same article to quote Origen, who said "[transcorporation is ... foreign to the Church of God and not handed down by the apostles or anywhere set forth in the scriptures." The testimonies of the Church Fathers, of a leading theosophist (Mead) and the least tortured interpretation of scripture, form an overwhelming argument against reincarnation as a doctrine of the early Church.

Reincarnationists apparently mistake early doctrinal squabbles as evidence that the church taught reincarnation in some form; for example, the doctrine of preexistence. This doctrine, which was taught by some of the church fathers, maintains that the soul existed somewhere in the spiritual cosmos prior to incarnation (birth) into the physical world. Reincarnationists take for their "proof" scripture that indicates that God knew us before we were born.

Reincarnationists also play games with resurrection doctrine and try to make it look either like a case of reincarnation or a mere semantic difference. They overlook the fact that resurrection occurs with the perfected version of the old body, not a different body; both Lazarus and Jesus were resurrected and both were resurrected in bodies recognized by people who knew them (such is not the case in reincarnation). Unfortunately, some Christians are guilty of fuzzy thinking on this score and believe that the two doctrines are somehow similar and compatible.

The Reincarnationist's World View

Although most people who believe in reincarnation and Karma are genuinely nice people, the overall world view produced by their belief is ultimately fatalistic and often produces a profound lack of concern for the suffering of others. One only has to look at India, a nation where reincarnation doctrine has reigned supreme for nearly three millenia, to see the tragic effects of that doctrine.

India is rich in resources but also has immense poverty and suffering. In a country where humans starve to death or suffer serious malnutrition and nutrionally related diseases, cows are sacred and cannot be used for food. The caste system, outlawed only in comparitively recent times, was oppressive in the extreme. Concern for others has traditionally been minimal in India and human life is cheap. Medical aid for all but the rich was almost nonexistent until Christian missionaries started coming to India in large numbers and set up clinics. All over the world, compassionate Christians often provided the first hope for the poor. Our missionaries have not been without some terrible faults but they were usually better than local leaders.

It has been claimed that Christians disdain death,

while the reincarnationist disdains life. Gandhi once remarked that reincarnation was a "burden too great to bear." Nowhere was reincarnationist disdain for life more evident than in the Nazi death camps. The men of the SS who carried out the crimes against the Jews (and others) originally were not brutes. Prior to joining the SS, most of them were good middle-class Lutheran and Roman Catholic youths. The SS took those clean-cut young people from their nominally Christian homes and taught them to commit murder. The SS men were indoctrinated with Hitler's theosophical beliefs about reincarnation and the Law of Karma.

The theosophically oriented Nazis believed that the Jews were a remnant of an earlier "root race" which preceded the present root race, which is called the "Aryan" race. This remnant, they were taught, defiles the Aryan race and inhibits its evolutionary ascent. When the SS man stuffed Jewish victims into the gas chambers, he honestly believed that he was engaged in something like vermin control; distasteful, repulsive but necessary. The SS killers were taught that causing Jewish victims to suffer, actually helped them in the long run by aiding them in working off a "racial Karmic debt." The Jewish soul, after an appropriate period of suffering, would then be able to reincarnate into a higher root race later on.

What power ideas possess! A good Lutheran boy or Catholic, raised with normal European values, is made into a murderer capable of the most heinous mass murders by the notion that he is cleansing the race. The irony is compounded by the belief that his victims were ultimately better off for having suffered.

The SS killers were part of an elite paramilitary organization that believed itself set aside by "Providence" for a special task in history. Their *esprit*

de corp was magnified by the belief that they were periodically reincarnated together at various times in history to fight the "Jewish menace." Their belief was
that the SS formed a small corp of cosmic warriors for
ages chasing the Jews down the corridors of history.

The suffering of the masses in India and the Holocaust of Europe is the legacy of the reincarnation and
Karma doctrines. That fact alone should give reincarnationists pause for concern. It does no good for New
Agers to put the Christians on a guilt trip over events
such as the Inquisition. Such crimes were carried out
by corrupted churchmen who distorted and twisted
the teachings of Christ. The crimes of the SS and the
status of India's poor are the logical result of reincar-
nation/Karma doctrine. That's a big difference!

Philosophical Basis of Reincarnation and the Law of Karma

Reincarnation and Karma are religious ideas
(despite claims to the contrary by some proponents of
reincarnation) and as such are inseparable from the
world view that generated the ideas. Claims of com-
patibility with Christianity fall under the weight of
the reincarnationist's philosophical baggage; the
world views represented by reincarnation and Christianity are mutually exclusive.

In the Christian world view, God is personal. He is
not merely a force of the universe; He is all powerful,
omniscient, omnipresent and merciful. He provided
for the salvation of fallen man through the death of
his son, Jesus. The penalty for our sin is death and
God elected to pay that penalty himself by incarnating
into human form and allowing His own execution.
In Christian belief, God created the universe but is
not identical with the universe; He is a separate being
who preexisted existence.

Reincarnation doctrine inevitably leads to a mon-

istic world view. Monism is the belief that all of Creation is ultimately of one substance. The monistic god
is not personal but, rather, is the universe itself. The
universe of the monist has consciousness of its own,
called the "Cosmic Consciousness" or the "Universal
Consciousness," which is said to be the Source of all
that Is; in other words, God.

The interesting implication in the monistic world
view is that God is not separate from His creation:
creation is God and God is creation. That belief logically leads us to conclude that everything in the universe is god: I am god, you are god, the dog is god and
so forth.

Reincarnationist doctrine is aligned with the
old gnostism but not with Christianity. Albrecht
tells us that there are four main attributes of gnostic
doctrine:

- Monism,
- The divinity of man,
- Gnosis as the main purpose of life and
- Mystical experience brings spiritual power.

The concept of monism is described above.

The "divinity of man" concept holds that, as a logical implication of monism, all men are divine beings.
As part of the universal divinity, man logically must
be divine himself. Our divinity is not apparent, however, because in our physical world we are too far removed from the godhead to perceive either its or our
own divinity. Our godhood is hidden as a tiny spark
deep inside of our soul somewhere, trapped in a deca-
dent physical body.

The purpose of our many lives is self-realization;
that is, to attain knowledge, direct experiential knowledge, of both God and our own inate divinity. This
knowledge is the *gnosis* of the ancient heretics and is
an idea that still lives. Attainment of sufficient

knowledge, or a high enough level of illumination, is the basis of salvation. Finally, after integrating the lessons of a million lifetimes, *gnosis* is complete and the soul achieves *nirvana* (extinction) or some other form of oneness with God.

The Western theory of evolution (Darwinism) is congenial to the reincarnationist. Mankind and individual souls are both said to be evolving upwards to higher levels of consciousness. Man's ascent up the evolutionary ladder is supposedly hurried by the practice of spiritual technologies. A soul that is particularly diligent can become a "Master of Wisdom," that is, a transhuman being who no longer requires reincarnation but has not quite yet reached godhood.

Finally, there is the claim that certain spiritual technologies lead to both spiritual power and further enlightenment. Disciplines such as yoga, asceticism, magical rituals and so forth supposedly bring this power. Eventually, the spiritual technologies lead one to merge more rapidly with God and the created becomes Creator.

"Proofs" of Reincarnation

A matter like reincarnation is notoriously difficult to prove so, as a result, reincarnationists go to extreme lengths to support their case. Researchers pile case upon case in an effort to shore up their sagging claims. Much reincarnation or ("past lives") research is done by people who lack any qualifications whatsoever or who tend to ignore the basic rules of evidence required of any scholar. Only a few researchers have both the qualifications and the integrity to conduct past lives research.

Professor Ian Stevenson of the University of Virginia is one such researcher, yet the title of his book (*Twenty Cases Suggestive of Reincarnation*)[12] reflects the immense difficulty of proof in his field of research.

Almost all reincarnation studies rely on "retrocognition" to prove the hypothesis. Retrocognition is defined as knowledge of past events, people or places, when there is no rational basis for the individual possessing such knowledge. If there is no other explanation, then retrocognition is cited.

An example of retrocognition was provided by a listener who called in to a radio talk show dealing with reincarnation. The woman claimed to have recalled in a vision the sights and smells of 18th-century Prague, Czechoslovakia. When she investigated her dream with a reincarnationist, she discovered that her dream provided accurate, detailed knowledge of the Prague street plan. This experience led the woman to believe that she had once lived as a Czechoslovakian Jewish woman in the 18th century.

There are three forms of retrocognition reported in reincarnationist literature; the woman's dream is but one of them. The three forms are *spontaneous recall*, *hypnotic regression* and *rebirthing therapy*. The experience of the woman cited before was an example of spontaneous recall.

Spontaneous recall operates automatically without apparent intervention of either the person involved or other persons. The recall of a past life comes in a vision, a dream or while fully awake in a kind of sudden knowing. Reincarnationists regard spontaneous recall as the most reliable research method.

In hypnotic regression, a second person hynotizes the subject and then works him backwards through subconscious memories that allegedly indicate past lives. Surprisingly detailed information about historically verified persons, places and events can be dredged up through hypnotic regression techniques.

Although hynotic regression is both easily done and very popular, there are some sound objections to the method. Not the least of which is the fact that hy-nosis by untrained people is potentially very danger-ous; some people regard any hypnosis as dangerous regardless of the training of the hypnotist.

Another objection to hynotic regression is that it is hardly ever a neutral process. In most cases, both the hynotist and the subject are either believers in rein-carnation or predisposed to belief prior to the session. There is a great deal of coaching from the hypnotist, so one needs to ask questions regarding pollution of the data obtained. Is the experience reported a genu-ine case of retrocognition or is it merely a response to suggestions of the hypnotist?

Rebirthing therapy is a newer technique and is not always related specifically to "past-lives" research. Al-though the technique is new enough that it is in a state of flux regarding details, there are certain com-monalities.

I interviewed a "Rebirthing Therapist" at a New Age retreat center north of Baltimore, Maryland. She told me that she has the subject lay down on a soft mattress or water bed and listen to a combination of "white noise" (hissing sounds) and soft music on a pair of stereo earphones. The idea seems to be genera-tion of spontaneous recall by technological means. There is some question whether Rebirthing Therapy is actually another form of hypnotism, rather than something new, even though my interviewee claimed that the method is not hypnotism in any form.

Still another form of Rebirthing Therapy uses vis-ualization to regress the subject back to past lives. When combined with talk therapy there is little dif-ference between rebirthing and the supposedly "Christian" Healing of Memories.

Both hypnotism and Rebirthing Therapy suffer a

general defect and that is the financial involvement of the hypnotist or therapist; both are providers of commercial services in most cases. The need to give clients "something for their money" either consciously or subconciously taints the results. Given that the hypnotist or therapist is financially involved, that both parties tend toward belief in the system and the experiences seem so real to the subject, it is little wonder that these methods are often enthusiastically touted as "proof" of reincarnation.

All forms of retrocognition suffer a fatal flaw because they are based on a false premise. The implied assumption is that cognition of past events, especially unexplained cognition, means that the person was present when the event took place. As we shall see later, having detailed knowledge of past events does not in any way mean that the person was present to witness those events.

Explanations of Retrocognition

Retrocognition is usually cited as proof of reincarnation, although reincarnation is but one possible explanation of the phenomenon. There are at least eight other explanations: *fraud, cryptoamnesia, genetic memory, extrasensory perception (ESP), personation, demon possession, spirit communications* and *mediumship*.[13]

Fraud. The possibility of fraud cannot be dismissed. Reincarnation is both profitable for the unscrupulous and romantic enough to attract victims to the con artist. Those two factors are a powerful combination that is just right for corruption. Charlatans find a rich market for their regression and rebirthing services.

Also under the "fraud" rubric might be unintentional fraud, even though that particular word combination is unpalatable (how can it be "fraud" if it is "unintentional?"). Such a case might come about when both parties sincerely want to find a past life. The effort then becomes something like a self-fulfilling prophecy. Neither party consciously intends deception but, by pre-biasing their attitudes, the results are consistent with expectations.

The possibility of untentional fraud is present in all scientific and scholarly research and must be guarded against. In medicine, for example, the expectations of the researcher and the patient can affect the apparent performance of a new experimental drug. The effects are not necessarily faked but are tainted one way or the other. This phenomena is the reason why medical researchers use control groups and double blind research protocols.

Under such a system, there will be two or more groups of patients. One group takes the real drug, while the second takes a neutral substance. In some cases, there are three groups: one for the new drug, one for a neutral substance and one for an older drug used to treat the same disease. Neither the patients, nor the nurses who administer the drugs, nor the physicians who evaluate the patients afterwards, know what patient is getting which pill. Unfortunately, reincarnation does not lend itself to double-blind studies, so unintentional fraud becomes a lot more likely.

Cryptoamnesia. The phenomenon of "cryptoamnesia" covers the case where a person learns something about the past, stores the knowledge in the subconscious mind but forgets it on the conscious level. The hidden knowledge is later dredged up during a hypnotic regression or rebirthing session or is spontaneously recalled and identified as past-life recall.

The celebrated Bridey Murphy case was an example of cryptoamnesia. In that case, a Colorado housewife was regressed and she revealed detailed knowledge of Ireland and talked with an Irish brogue during those sessions. Because the woman had never been to Ireland to learn the accent and since she had never been a student of Irish culture, "Bridey Murphy" was touted as a case of reincarnation.

Even some normally skeptical scientists accepted "Bridey Murphy" as genuine. Later, more careful investigators revealed that the woman had an Irish grandmother who had told her much about the old homeland and she spoke in a thick Irish brogue. This knowledge was planted in the woman's subconscious as a very young child and it came out later during a hypnotic regression session as an adult.

Earlier I mentioned a radio talk show where a woman caller claimed to have shown detailed knowledge of Prague, Czechoslovakia, its street plan and Jewish culture in the city. She accepted her dream as evidence of having lived once before as an 18th-century Czechoslovakian Jewish woman. I suggest cryptoamnesia as a possible — even probable — alternate explanation of her experience. The radio talk show was "The Fred Fisk Show" on WAMU-FM in Washington, D.C. during August 1984; the show was hosted not by Fisk but by an alternate emcee who seemed congenial towards reincarnation. The woman claimed that her experience took place a few months earlier.

During the previous December ("... a few months earlier!") the Smithsonian Institution in Washington, D.C., hosted an exhibit titled *The Precious Legacy,* which was a collection of antique Judaica from the Jewish Museum in Prague, Czechoslovakia.[14] The collection was originally put together by slave curators under the Nazi regime and consisted of treasures and memorabilia stolen by the Nazis from the Jews and their synagogues. The Nazis' purpose was to open a "museum to an extinct race."

My wife and I stood in line with our bored children for two hours to see *The Precious Legacy* exhibit. Media in Washington, D.C., the city where the woman caller lived and had her dream, was full of Holocaust stories during the winter 1983-84; reports of the Smithsonian exhibition were very much in the news. It is possible that the woman dredged up memories of the exhibit and misidentified it as a past life experience. One of the exhibit items was a gray-tone street map of Prague in an earlier century!

Keep in mind that cryptoamnesia is not fraudulent for the subject honestly does not remember learning the information that comes out as retrocognition.

Genetic Memory. This explanation is popular with certain people but I am skeptical about it. It is claimed that certain memories are somehow stored in our cell DNA and can be decoded by the brain under some circumstances. Genetic memory is passed on from parent to child in a manner similar to hair color and facial features. Supporters of this theory point to seemingly instinctive behavior as evidence. Unless physicians, life scientists and psychologists become generally convinced of this theory and can explain it to me, I will discount it.

Extrasensory Perception (ESP). This explanation is popular with those people who prefer a "natural" explanation of retrocognition. ESP phenomena fall under the quasi-scientific rubric of "parapsychology" and are regarded as natural occurances about which we know little. The ESP explanation is not mystical but natural. Parapsychologists disdain the labels "occult" and "supernatural" so may attempt to explain retrocognition as a mind-reading exercise or some other ESP phenomenon.

Demon possession. It is amazing how many people refuse to believe in the possibility of demonic possession. Even some Christian clergymen scorn the possibility of demon possession, despite the fact that the Bible is very specific on that point. Although one must be cautious about claims of demon possession and must certainly not label every bit of unusual behavior as evidence of demonism, the possibility of demon possession must be recognized.

Why would a possessing evil spirit want to deceive the subject regarding past lives? The answer is that demons want to keep humans from salvation. By convincing people of the "reality" of reincarnation, they turn those people away from the offer of salvation by grace. Reincarnation is touted as an alternate means of salvation, so the soul is lost for the belief in a false system.

The information provided by retrocognition through a demon possessed person should be quite authentic. Time is almost meaningless to spirit beings so they would have witnessed those past people, places and events and reported on them through the subject.

Spirit Communications. Apart from demon possession, there is also the possibility that evil spirit beings will attempt to plant "proof" of reincarnation into the mind of a subject through one or another means of communication. The remark of Sir John Eccles, "the brain is a machine a ghost can operate," takes on immense significance.

Mediumship and Altered Consciousness. The medium goes into a trance in order to contact disincarnate beings. In the altered state of consciousness, dreams and visions are very vivid and may lead to misinterpretation by the subject. If cross-checking is not diligently done, then a researcher may well succumb to the vision and accept it as valid.

Personation. This phenomenon occurs when an individual closely identifies with a another person and either learns or fabricates details of that person's life and environment well enough to render credible accounts to an uncritical audience. Personation is not fraud but more nearly like cryptoamnesia and, in fact, may combine with cryptoamnesia.

Reincarnation vs. Resurrection

The usual ploy of writers trying to prove reincarnation is to pile case history upon case history. Such tactics are the only methods open to them, given the impossibility of absolute proof in any form of life-after-death research. Unfortunately for their position, piling up large numbers of soft cases as evidence is no more convincing than showing but one such case. After all, error plus error does not equal truth. One hundred-thousand speculative "could-be" cases are still "could-be" cases and do not lend each other weight, except in the uncritical mind. One confirmed case (if reincarnation were confirmable) would be infinitely superior to the mass of unconfirmed speculative evidence now offered.

Christians reject reincarnation and instead teach resurrection of the dead. The resurrected body will be the same person as before, would be seen by eyewitnesses and a record would be made of such an astounding event. The resurrected dead are not the same as the medically resuscitated or so-called "clinically dead." Experiences reported by those people are interesting psychologically and religiously but do not represent a true life-after-death experience; only a near-death experience. Those people were not really dead.

Philosopher Tal Brooke proposes a test in his book

The Other Side of Death.[15] The "Lazarus Test" of resurrection refers to the story of Lazarus in the Gospels. The dead man was in the tomb four days and his body had begun to decompose when Jesus resurrected him. The Lazarus Test requires the onset of decomposition and thus would nicely differentiate true resurrections from mere resuscitations.

The resurrection of Lazarus was witnessed by numbers of people and recorded in the New Testament. But the Lazarus event was neither the only nor the most important resurrection in the Bible. The Gospels record the most important event for mankind in all of history: the resurrection of Jesus. The Lazarus Test was met in Jesus' resurrection for Jesus was in the tomb for three days. Furthermore, He was seen after his resurrection by large numbers of eyewitnesses and the event was recorded in writing (the Gospels) for the benefit of future generations.

Lawyers have examined the Gospels with the purpose of building a case against their authenticity, only to become converted themselves. They came to belief when they realized that the evidence for the resurrection of Jesus is both sound and compelling and in accordance with legal principles of evidence. The best evidence for the existence of an event is eyewitness accounts and the existence of so many eyewitnesses argues loudly for the case of resurrection. The case is made all the stronger by the fact that so many eyewitnesses were willing to die for their belief. A few people might be crazy enough to die for a lie, as might later believers who were not eyewitnesses and came to believe a myth — but not scores upon scores of people who witnessed the events and knew the truth.

It appears that some New Agers also recognize that eyewitnesses are the best evidence for the Christian case. When they admit resurrection at all, they almost inevitably deny or fail to mention that Jesus walked through the countryside for more than a month after his resurrection showing himself to many eyewitnesses. The typical New Age response to Christian claims might be that it was not a real, physical body but rather a phantasmic "ethereal" body that was seen (Jesus was a ghost?). Of course, that argument crumbles in the face of Thomas' testimony. "Doubting Thomas" wanted to feel the wounds in Jesus body — how can one feel wounds on a phantasm?

Conclusion

We have given Reincarnation and the Law of Karma doctrines a fair hearing and found them wanting. They are unproven, philosophically flawed and quite unsupportable. They are totally incompatible with Christian belief. Nevertheless, large numbers of people will continue to believe in them — more than 60 million Americans by some accounts. Unfortunately, the ultimate reward for such belief is eternal damnation — a terribly high price to pay for an erroneous world view.

3

Occultism:

Gateway to the New Age

For many people the doorway to the New Age is old-fashioned occultism. By peeking into a titillating hidden corner they become ensnared in a much larger and ultimately hideous domain. Occultism is the study of hidden (spiritual) things. Interest in the occult has increased to such an extent that today the Church can no longer ignore it. One source claims that one-fourth of all Americans are involved in at least some aspect of occultism. Even segments of the Church, some knowingly, others in ignorance, teach one or more occultic doctrines in the guise of enlightened Christianity.[1]

Although occultism has been with us since before the time of Babylon, the modern emphasis began in earnest early in the 19th century. The "Occult Revival" was a major force in Western culture at that time.[2] During the decades when Christianity declined in Europe, occultism revived as a counterculture answer to atheistic science and the philosophy of materialism which science represented.

Many people were ill at ease with the scientific world view but for a variety of reasons they were also disillusioned with the Church. The Occult Revival both met their immediate spiritual needs and provided them with fantastic, entertaining experi-

47

ences. It also provided them with a sense of belong-
ingness in that occultism represented an intimate cult
of those who accepted knowledge that the rest of society rejected.[3]

The Church's response to occultism has been woefully inadequate. Very few of our leaders can accurately state what the word "occultism" means. For example, one of the leading Christian authorities on cults
and occultism wrote one of the standard reference
works on the subject.[4] In it, he lists under "Occultism"
such topics as astrology, palmistry and Tarot cards. Yet
the principal occultic movements (e.g., theosophy
and others) are merely "cults." The matters which
that author calls "occult" are certainly part of it but
only a small part. They are merely tools, methods and
modalities used in a much larger context.

Permit me to explain by way of an example. If astrology (etc.) are all of occultism, then the church or-
gan is all of Christianity.

One reason for the Church's inept response to occultism is the teaching that Christians should
avoid negative things. This unfortunate attitude is an
outgrowth of the positive thinking movement,
which as you will see is part of the problem, not the
solution. Many people in the Church have a false
idea of how we should examine occultism (and similar matters).

Often used is the woefully inadequate metaphor
regarding counterfeit money. The claim is made that
the U.S. Secret Service teaches moneyhandlers to recognize counterfeit currency by concentrating only on
genuine currency. The implication of this metaphor
is that we should bury our heads in the sand. Supporters of this view misuse the truth that we need to
keep our eyes on Jesus and never examine anti-
Christian movements. Isn't it sad how that the

Church is the only army that despises intelligence reports on the enemy!

The "counterfeit currency" metaphor is as false as the lesson it teaches. The Secret Service teller-training material does, in fact, concentrate on the features of genuine currency — but it also shows common examples of counterfeit currency so that the teller will learn to recognize the common errors made by counterfeiters. The idea behind that material is to teach the points of recognition for both genuine and counterfeit. In the same manner we need to examine the principal errors in occultism and the major heresies.

Poor use is also made of scripture passages such as Romans 16:19, which teaches: " … but I want you to be wise in what is good and *innocent* of what is evil." The word "innocent" is taken to mean that we should totally ignore cults and occultism, that is, to have no knowledge of them at all. Perhaps the proper meaning is that we should not participate in these things. Basing opinion on single verses — i.e. "proof texting" — frequently leads to error that would be eliminated by the testimony of the whole passage, indeed of all of scripture. Verse 17 of Romans 16, after all, admonishes us to *keep our eyes on the false teachers so that we may be wary of them* — and Isaiah admonishes us to set watchmen on the wall.

What Is Occultism?

The word "occult" is derived from Latin and refers to things that are hidden, secret or mysterious.[5] This meaning does not refer to things that are merely presently unknown but are ultimately knowable through ordinary means (i.e., the five senses). It refers instead to matters that transcend our ordinary senses. Included in this category are a whole range of phenomena and practices, only some of which were

mentioned above. We can make the following state-ments regarding occultism; it deals with:
- Things that are hidden, concealed or secret;
- Events, beings, entities, processes or phenomena that are beyond the abilities of the five senses;
- Superhuman powers and
- Supernatural (both angelic and demonic) forces.

There are many aspects to occultism, almost (it seems) custom tailored to fit the needs, moods and desires of all people. There are, however, four general catagories to consider; others are subsets of the follow-ing: *divination, magick* (note spelling), *spiritism* and *mys-ticism.*[6]

Divination

Divination is the occultic practice by which a per-son can by supernatural means predict future events, predict human character, see at a distance current events, find lost objects or substances (e.g. water) or tap into the past to actually "witness" historic events. There are several subsets to divination including for-tune telling, palmistry and others. We will deal with these and others shortly. But first, let's discuss what divination is not.

Divination is not clairvoyance. Although some people claim a degree of prescience (ability to see the future), there is a different quality to such reported ex-periences and no intent. Clairvoyance, if it actually exists (which is by no means proven), is a spontane-ous and often unwanted intrusion on consciousness.

There is another definition of clairvoyance used in conjunction with spiritism but more of that later.

Divination, on the other hand, is prescience by in-tent. The diviner (practicer of divination) uses tranc-es, spirit contacts, omens, astrology, ouija boards or other allegedly magical objects such as cards, pendulums, palmlines or the entrails of sacrificed animals to make predictions of the future.[7]

Divination also is not prophecy. There are three aspects to genuine prophecy — admonition (or rebuke), exhortation and prescience — and the common thread running through all three is that God's word is manifest. Like clairvoyance, prophecy is rarely sought and — given the treatment historically meted out to biblical prophets by their own people — often unwanted. Unlike clairvoyance, prophecy is known to exist and will never contradict or "clarify" scripture.

After we exclude all cases where divination is used for entertainment purposes and for which no serious claim is pressed for genuiness, we are left with a residue of instances where some form of prescience occurs (or at least appears to occur). There are five possible explanations for such events: fraud, psychology, ESP, divine intervention and demonic intervention.[8]

Fraud. In cases of fraudulent divination there is no reality to the events and their source is human deception. These cases are distinquished from entertainment illusions because of the intent of the perpetrators. Also included in this catagory are cases where the diviner is not fully aware of his intent to deceive until systematically questioned. In those sad cases even the diviner is deceived.

Psychology. Cases of this type have no supernatural basis but are rather manifestations of someone's overactive psyche. Whatever the complexities of the case, however, the phenomenon is founded in either a distorted world view or some misfiring neurons.

Extrasensory Perception (ESP). This explanation may or may not be valid depending upon the reality of ESP phenomena. The ESP explanation would, like the psychological, be naturalistic. I remain skeptical of ESP and give it consideration only because the evidence is inconclusive. While the cynic may claim that ESP is false because evidence is both inconclusive and often contradictory, the proper position to take is cautious recognition of its possible truth. Inconclusive evidence serves for neither acceptance nor rejection of ESP phenomena. Caution is the watchword, however, for ESP may turn out to be ultimately demonic. And given the unbiblical context of most ESP "readings," probably is demonic.

Divine Intervention. God or his angelic agents on His command, could conceivably intervene in human affairs by means of diviners, for He is sovereign — but I doubt that He would do it. The universal test of divine revelation is the "Rule of Contradiction." If the revealed information contradicts, modifies or denies prior biblical revelation then it is false. My opinion regarding God using diviners, apart from episodes of genuine prophecy, stems from a reading of Deuteronomy 18. The question raised by Deuteronomy 18 is: Would God act through a means that He expressly forbids us to use? I doubt it.

Demonic Intervention. All of our previous categories are relatively benign. We must now consider the possibility of demonic intervention as the explanation for occultic phenomena; demonic influence is always malignant, never benign. Because the demonic explanation is the most serious (and in my view most probable), we will assume that all forms of divination that cannot be explained naturalistically are demonic in origin.

Why would demons take delight in deceiving man through divination and other occult practices? Although there are undoubtedly many variations on the demonic theme, the root reason is to turn people away from God. Their abiding interest is to switch your allegiance from the Creator to the created.

Aspects of Divination

The particular practices that make up the art of divination are varied and many. Most of them have one or more of the following goals:

- Foreseeing events,
- Discerning a person's character,
- Finding lost objects, people or substances,
- Seeing at a distance and
- Postviewing (i.e. seeing events in the past).

There are any number of variants of the occult technologies used in these forms of divination; some of them are used over a broad range of goals. Some of the most common occult technologies are described below.[9]

Astrology. This occult technology is based on the erroneous belief that a person's character and "fate" is determined by, influenced by or discernible from the positions of the sun, moon, stars and planets at the moment of birth. Astrology originated during the third millenium B.C. (or earlier) when it was practiced by Chaldean and Babylonian priests. Although astrology was once wedded with the science of astronomy and may have actually spawned scientific astronomy, it is not part of any science today. Astrology is practiced in variations by almost all peoples, with remarkable similarities among widespread sources.

Cartomancy (Tarot). Cartomancy is a form of divination in which special playing cards, called "Tarot cards," are used to see into the future. The Tarot deck consists of cards of different designs, each of which has a special meaning. Additional meaning is conferred by placement of the cards and by juxtaposition of different types of cards. The history of Tarot cards dates back to the first century A.D. and they may have been introduced into Europe in the 13th century.

Related forms of cartomancy include bone reading used by primitive shaman and runestone reading by pre-Christian Norsemen. In these cases, symbols are inscribed on bone or small baked clay tablets instead of paper playing cards.

Chiromancy (Palmistry). Chiromantists claim that a person's future and character are revealed by lines and "mounds" in the palms of the hands. Palmists claim that there are four lines (heart, life, head and fate) and seven "planet mounds" (Mercury, Apollo, Saturn, Venus, Jupiter, Mars and Moon). The combination and geometry of these features supposedly reveal the character and fate of the person. Some sources date palmistry as far back as early Babylon, although a date of Roman times is more reasonable.

Glass Manticy. Also called crystal ball gazing, this form of divination attempts to discern the future (or see at a distance) through gazing into a rock crystal (quartz) ball, still water, mirror or any of several "sacred" natural mineral crystals (quartz family crystals are said to be especially effective).

Psychometry. The art of psychometry is divination through psychic examination of an object a person has either worn, touched or used. Psychometry has been used with indifferent success to locate lost persons, lost objects and by police to solve crimes.

Numerology. This discipline dates back to Babylonian times and claims ability to discern truths about a person from the number of his name. All letters of the alphabet are assigned a numerical value, so any word or name has an equivalent numerical value equal to the sum of the letter values. Numerology is probably the basis for the "number of his name" (666) prophecy in Revelation regarding anti-christ.

Postviewing. Occultists claim the ability to look back into the past psychically in order to see what actually happened. According to this theory, the records of the past and future are stored in the universal (or "cosmic") consciousness and stretch out from past through the present to the future like a scarlet ribbon. Under the right circumstances, such as a mystical trance, the occultist claims the ability to read these so-called "Akashic records."

The above are merely broad areas of divination and the list is not intended to be complete. There are assorted systems that depend on reading such things as tea leaves, smoke curls, bones, entrails of sacrificed animals, omens and such.

Magick

Magick is a part of occultism and, according to some authorities, the most bizarre aspect. Occultic magick is different from stage magic (note spelling difference). The stage magician uses deception, trickery and illusion to entertain the audience and makes no serious claim to either special powers or supernatural intervention.

Occultic magick is quite different and can be defined as the *attempt to control, rule or know both natural and supernatural worlds by supernatural means, through the use of special ceremonies, rituals, rites, objects or words that in and of themselves possess power.*[10] A related (and nearly synonomous) word is "sorcery."

The word "magick" was allegedly coined by Aliester Crowley to differentiate ritual magic from the stage variety ("magic"). Crowley was once called "the wickedest man alive" and he vowed to break every moral law known to man. According to some sources he very nearly succeeded.[11]

Two forms of magick are recognized: personal and natural. Personal magick supposedly calls on disincarnate spirit beings — demons — in order to effect the result desired from the ritual. The magus (ritual magician) uses incantations and rituals to appeal to, cajole, influence or control the demonic beings who supposedly bring about the result.

Few magi will admit that the intelligences which they invoke are demonic. Indeed, many of them believe the beings are either neutral or angelic. The demonic nature of the beings becomes evident from reading Deuteronomy 18:9-12. If magick is forbidden by God, then angels will not react to supplications of a magical nature.

Natural magick is based on the premise that supernatural control is possible through an understanding of subtle "laws of the universe" that are unknown to the majority of man. It is supposedly possible to supernaturally control physical events through the rituals of magick by influence on purely natural forces. Although we must by no means assume that we understand all of the laws of nature, it is highly improbable that such will ever be found that responds to words of incantation and other magical exotica.

Methods of Magick

Rites, rituals and ceremonies are essentially the same sort of event and are supposedly the vehicle for contacting the beings or forces who cause the desired result. The forms of ritual vary considerably from one system to another but there are some commonalities. The main methods of magick are: invocation, casting spells (charming), symbolic ritual and the use of fetishes.[12]

Invocation involves the repeating of words or rites that either appeal to or command (depending upon the system) a supernatural being. The being invoked may be demonic or angelic, god or devil or some allegedly neutral spirit being. In so-called "Christian" systems of magick the being is supposed to be either God, Jesus, the Holy Spirit, the Virgin Mary or some other personality. In pagan systems, it might be the goddesses Isis or Ishtar, a less distinct mother goddess or some animistic deity. Other systems invoke certain metaphysical beings such as Lord Maitreya or some deceased human.

Spell casting or "charming" involves words or rituals that bring the forces of nature against the problem at hand. Charming differs from invocation in that natural forces rather than personalities are invoked. The spell may be as benign as attempting to confer good luck on a person or as malignant as voodoo death spells. Some sources use the word "charming" to denote hypnotism, which may explain why such spells seem to work.

Symbolic rituals are acts, events, rituals, dances, movements and other physical practices that supposedly empower magical attempts.

Fetishes are physical objects that are supposedly charged with magical power. Included under this definition are talismans, good luck charms, bones, amulets, gemstones, medallions and so forth. Depending upon the system of magick, almost any physical object or animal can be made into a fetish.

Magick falls under the general category of sorcery. Two words are translated "sorcery" in scripture: *magia* and *pharmakeia*. The latter is the root of the word "pharmacy" and may refer to the taking of drugs to alter the state of consciousness in order to gain mystical experiences. The popular psychedelic drugs of the 1960s produced this effect, as does mescaline (peyote).

The other word for sorcery is *magia* which refers to the type of ritual discussed in this section. All forms of sorcery are condemned in scripture.

White Magick vs. Black Magick

There are many occultists who honestly believe that they are not practicing evil with their magick. They attempt to distinquish between so-called "white magick" and "black magick." White magick supposedly does not seek to harm anyone or gain any unfair advantage over them and is rarely used to personal benefit by the magician.

Black magick is just the opposite. According to this view, black magick is the form that either seeks personal gain or to harm others in some way. Scripture, however, uses no adjectives — all forms of sorcery are condemned.

The practice of "manifestation" is a magical means for acquiring material goods.[13] In August 1984 I heard a top New Age spiritual teacher claim that he became a writer and had to "manifest" (i.e., conjure) a typewriter. A former New Age occultist who is now a Christian told me that she "visualized" (an occultic technique) a yellow Volkswagen and other goods.[14] Many users of these techniques testify that they work and work well.

Let's reconsider the definition of magick (*magia* or sorcery). Restated, it is the attempt to control the natural and supernatural worlds by supernatural means through the use of rituals, techniques or words that *in and of themselves have power*. Thus, the practice of manifestation is sorcery or magick, regardless of whether occultic visualization or "words of power" are used by the magician. Furthermore, by the definition given earlier, its selfish goal makes it black magick.

Christian Magick

When referring to so-called "Christian" magick in this present context we mean sorcery practiced by saved Christians. We are not referring to the practices of others who merely claim to be Christian but rather attempts by believing Christians — born again people who practice magick.

Let's first point out that such people do not usually know that they are practicing forbidden magick. Instead, they believe that God — through the Holy Spirit more often than not — is granting a supernatural favor or assistance. God does, after all, help His people and that help is sometimes material things miraculously obtained. It is also true that God is true to His word, and He will answer our prayers according to His own wisdom. I have only a few problems with most faith teachers, but with a few their teaching is so wrong that comment is necessary.

There is a substantial difference between magick and prayer. Prayer is an appeal, a supplication made in humility with the expectation of being happy with whatever answer God gives (and "no" is a valid answer). Magick, on the other hand, attempts to command God to provide the desired goods. Some of the "faith teaching" heard today is little more than an attempt at forbidden magick. A few of the "Name It And Claim It" teachers have stepped over a very broad doctrinal line by claiming that God is required to obey your desires when you use the right words. Furthermore, some even maintain that the *words used to invoke God's pleasure are powerful in and of themselves,* and will work regardless of whether or not the person uttering them is a Christian. That's black magick no matter how famous the preacher who teaches this heresy. Compare the doctrine taught by some Christians on the fringes of the Church with the "manifestation" teaching of occultists: They are the same.

Spiritism

Spiritism, also called "spiritualism" and "necromancy," is the attempt to make contact with the dead. According to this belief, the spirits of the dead are capable of making contact with the living through various means. Some authorities distinquish "spiritism" from "spiritualism" on grounds that spiritualists often claim to be Christian, while spiritists do not. This distinction is partially true but not absolutely. Many non-Christian necromancers call themselves by both names. For the sake of simplicity, in this book we will use the term "spiritism" to denote all forms of necromancy.[15]

Spiritism exists in a number of guises. For some it is not a serious matter but rather is a diversionary activity. For others it is a formal religion with "churches," schools and other furniture associated with formally established religions. Although spiritism dates back to the book of Exodus, its modern form began in 1847 in the upstate New York town of Hydeville. The John D. Fox family moved into a house formerly occupied by one Charles Posma, who supposedly had been murdered. The two Fox daughters, Margaret and Kate, began to hear knockings and rappings in the house. Subsequently, fragments of a human skeleton were found in the cellar of the house and that find established the girl's credibility.[16]

The Fox sisters publicly admitted in 1886 that their "experiences" were fraudulent, although both later repudiated their confessions. Nevertheless, the spiritist movement remains popular worldwide. Missionaries reporting from Brazil tell us that spiritism is one of the largest religious groups in that country.

Although popular for years among certain fringe elements, modern spiritism gained a certain respectibility when Episcopal Bishop James Pike began to practice the forbidden art. The story of Pike's necromancy is told in Merrill Unger's book, *The Haunting of Bishop Pike*.[17] Pike's interest was fueled by grief over the suicide death of his son and was sparked by a chain of apparently ghostly happenings. Bishop Pike died while wandering lost on the Judaean desert, some years after his Christian faith died on a desert of unbelief.

The basic supposition of spiritism is that some essence of the human being, usually said to be either the soul or the spirit, survives death and lingers about the physical world in an unseen parallel spirit world. In classical spiritism that unseen world is called Summerland, while in more recent New Age terminology it is called the Ethereal or Astral Plane.

According to most spiritists, Summerland is a pleasant place and is not to be feared. They testify that there is no heaven or hell in the Christian sense of the terms. Those who believe in reincarnation sometimes claim that Summerland is one of the non-physical planes on which the soul rests between incarnations.[18] According to certain New Age teachings the plane called "Summerland" by spiritists is the location of hell but is not a permanent residence of the soul. According to this view, the sinner's soul suffers a while on the Astral Plane before being elevated — after some "bad karma" is worked off — to a higher plane.

Although the "beings" who "come through" by way of channeling (seances) are reportedly benign, others report that various beings haunt the Astral

Plane/Summerland and some of them are terribly evil. Christians should understand that all of them are evil. Those who appear good or benign, are actually evil spirits counterfeiting the experience to lead people astray.

Although several modalities for contacting spirits are practiced by spiritists, perhaps the most famous is the medium or "channeler" (as New Agers would have it). Such persons are said to have an extraordinary sensitivity to the spirit world. Although people who claim to be channels usually deny that they are mediums, there is little or no real difference between the two types of necromancer — and both are engaged in forbidden trafficking with demons. The only apparent difference at all is that mediums claim to contact dead souls, exclusively, while channelers are less specific (or more eclectic) about who or what they contact (often it is the "Masters of Wisdom").

Although not universally true, mediums usually work in a trance. That is, they achieve an altered state of consciousness in which they seem to surrender control of their faculties to the spirit. Raphael Gasson, writing in *The Challenging Counterfeit*, tells us that the spirit takes full control of the medium's body and " ... the medium knows nothing whatever about the procedure of the seance, having to be told of the results when he regains consciousness."[19]

Of many types of trance mediums with a public following, perhaps the most famous was Edgar Cayce. Although his followers often deny that Cayce was a medium, he gave thousands of "readings" while in a sleep-like state that strongly resembled the mediumistic trance. Cayce's work is perpetuated by the Association for Research and Enlightenment in Virginia Beach, Virginia.

Methods of Mediums

The medium has several means for making contact with what he believes is the spirit world. Perhaps the most famous is the trance state. Depending upon the type of medium and his capabilities, the trance may be entered in either a darkened room or a normally lit room. Some means is generally used to "center down" and thereby force the onset of the trance state.

I once witnessed a trance medium operate at a pseudo-Christian New Age retreat center.[20] The young woman medium asked all people present to be quiet while she began to recite a repetitious "prayer" in an unknown (to me, at least) lanquage. I am not prepared to state flatly that she was not speaking a known ancient or modern language. The medium was seated between two assistants and all three of them prayed with their hands laid face up on their laps. After two or three minutes her body noticibly stiffened, her facial expression changed and her voice became hoarser. The "message" that followed the centering down process sounded a lot like prophecies heard in certain churches; a fact which should warn Christians to test all spirits in everything they say or do. After all, as the title of Gasson's book illustrates and scripture warns, Satan can and does counterfeit the miraculous.

Whether in a formal seance or in a less-formal situation such as I witnessed, the medium allows his or her body to be taken over (i.e., "overshadowed") by a "spirit" being — in other words a demon. Christians know that these beings are not the spirits of the dead but rather demons from hell impersonating the deceased.

Not all mediums use the formal trance or seance in its usual form. Some use one or more other techniques to record the words of the demon. An example is automatic writing. This form of alleged communication requires the use of a pen, pencil or typewriter. Presumedly, a modern word processor would open entire new vistas of electronic automatic writing.

Entire books and at least one TV show, by famous occultist authors, have been written using automatic writing.[21] The author sits poised with pencil (or whatever) in hand and on the paper until he or she feels it begin to move. Alternatively, the medium sits with fingers poised on the keyboard until they begin to twitch and spell out the message. Presumedly, the modern word processor opens up all kinds of possibilities for even lazy mediums. Given the nature of those electronic marvels, perhaps the medium can leave the word processor turned on, have the message electronically recorded and then check it from time to time as a kind of ghostly high-tech electronic mailbox.

Mysticism

The bottom line for many — perhaps most — New Age activities is mysticism. In order to understand the types of activities that are mystical in nature, let's develop the word from its root: *mystic.*

According to *Webster's New Collegiate Dictionary,* the word "mystic" is synonymous with "occult." The word "mystical," which means pertaining to the mystic, deals with those things that are "not apparent to the five senses," yet convey spiritual meaning of one sort or another. It is the fact that things mystical are beyond the five senses that links it to the occult.[22]

Mysticism deals with knowledge that is experientially derived, rather than intellectual knowledge. This experience is said to reveal the "Inner Light" or "Illumination." It is the experiential aspect that makes something mystical.

In line with the concept of experiential knowledge is the definition of mysticism from *Webster's:* "Belief that direct knowledge of God (i.e., gnosis, spiritual truth or ultimate reality can be obtained by intuition or insight). Further, mysticism is the belief that one can obtain " ... ineffable knowledge or power." Something "ineffable" is beyond the power of language to describe.

If mystical experiences are beyond the five senses and ineffable, then what is their nature and how are they attained? The answers to these questions will, perhaps, reveal why they are not recommended for Christians.

The nature of the mystical experiences is that they are either dredged up from some subconscious depths or are generated from some malfunctioning brain cells somewhere. Regardless of their origin or the techniques used to obtain them, mystical experiences open the mystic to possible demonic influences. We will discuss this matter in a moment.

Mystical experiences come through an altered state of consciousness. Although some of them come spontaneously, most such experiences result from an intentional effort on the part of the mystic. A variety of psychospiritual technologies are used to enter the altered state (also called the Shamanic State of Consciousness or SSC) including drugs, hyperventilation, yoga, variants of hypnosis, rhythmic dancing or music or biofeedback (among others).[23] The psychedelic experiences of the hippie generation were mystical in nature, a fact that explains why so many veterans of the drug subculture turned to the New Age, Eastern religions and occultism.

Biofeedback can be particularly insidious because outside the New Age it is not billed as a mystical technique but rather it is called "medical" or "scientific."

During one phase of my professional career I was a biomedical engineer in a university hospital and medical center (I hold a master of science degree in medical engineering). Partially because it was operated by the electrical engineering department, the program in our school was heavily slanted towards subjects related to alpha wave biofeedback. It struck me as odd that the majority of non-medical people who asked me to help them build alpha brainwave instruments for biofeedback were also involved in illegal drug use.

Alpha wave biofeedback is used to enter the so-called "alpha state" which we normally enter just as we fall asleep. A significant danger with alpha wave feedback is the potential for creating an epileptic seizure. The alpha class of brain waves is a natural electrical signal in the frequency range of eight to 13 cycles per second (cps). These signals can be detected with scalp electrodes connected to a suitable biopotentials amplifier.

The idea in biofeedback is to monitor your brainwaves through a special instrument that is connected to scalp electrodes embedded in a headband. The goal is to reinforce the alpha waves and suppress others until you can automatically enter the alpha state unassisted. The supposed benefits are reduction of mental stress and enhanced creativity (neither benefit is adequately proven scientifically).

The danger in alpha biofeedback is that certain sub-seizure level waveforms contain components in the same frequency band (8-13 cps). Latent epileptics, who have not yet exhibited seizure activity, may have these components unbeknown to themselves. So lack of prior seizure history is no indicator that the practice is alright for you. When you connect yourself to an alphawave monitor, as do thousands of New Age questors, it is possible that you will reinforce the alpha state as desired — it is also equally likely that you will reinforce an epileptic seizure and have the experience of your life!

Michael Harner, author of *The Way of the Shaman* and himself a practicing shaman, reveals that the shamanistic trance (SSC) is one and the same with the mystical experience.[24] Harner explains the use of the shaman's drum or rattle to produce the musical beat that aids the shaman (a type of witchdoctor, to use Western terminology) in entering the SSC. Certain forms of rock and New Age music seem to have a similar potential.[25]

Demonic Influences

The demonic never seems far away in mysticism. Reading the reports of mystics (there is a vast literature available on the subject) demonstrates three aspects that seem to indicate demonic activity. First, most of the entities encountered in the SSC seem to have an inordinate interest in Jesus Christ; an interest far too great if He is merely who or what they claim. Invariably, they tell us that Jesus was a great teacher, one of many Christs and that the church for selfish reasons has distorted the true doctrine.

Second, there is a tremendous sense of oneness with the universe and a feeling that the universe is God. This monism of the mystic is what got them in trouble (heresy) in all three transcendent religions: Islam, Judaism and Christianity. The monism produced by the mystical experience contradicts the lessons of scripture, which demonstrate that God is transcendent; i.e., separate from, outside and greater than His creation. If God was the universe and vice versa, then He would not be transcendent but rather immanent (another New Age claim).

Finally, there is also the fact that people who enter the SSC frequently come back terrified of what they saw "over there." In some primitive societies, the shaman always works with an assistant who will help pull him back into this world if something goes awry. The SSC can be entered by the technique called "visualization."

Read Johanna Michaelson's book *The Beautiful Side of Evil* for an account of her terrifying experiences in visualization.[26] Her testimony should be adequate for those who are tempted to try it, even in a Christian context (the use of visualization is an occultic technique but nonetheless has invaded the Church).

We are easily pursuaded that New Agers by the hundreds of thousands practice one or more techniques to attain the SSC. We need not look too far, for they are open and honest about the matter (even though not all of them call it mysticism). What is a little more difficult to see is Christian mysticism. Many thousands of honest Christians, including (perhaps particularly) pastors who should know better, indulge in mysticism. I once heard a report of a church that chanted "Jesus! Jesus! Jesus!" over and over again for an hour at a time. When some of the members had psychedelic experiences, the pastors held that the Holy Spirit was doing a mighty work. It was more likely a case of people entering the SSC by repetitive chanting and hyperventilation (an easily discerned New Age method, by the way). Churches that practice visualization are in direct violation of God's law and should reread Deuteronomy.

Fellow Christian author, Elissa McClain *(Rest From the Quest)*, knows a woman who came out of a form of New Age mysticism called "Wicca" (the proper name for witchcraft) and became a Christian.[27] She attended a certain (supposedly) charismatic church for three months before she knew there was a difference between it and Wicca! That's a terrible indictment of that pastor and I am glad that most charismatic assemblies don't fall into that trap.

The supposed justification for modern Christian mysticism is the famous mystics of past centuries. Historical figures such as Meister Eckart, Madame Guyon, Teresa of Avila and John of the Cross are highly regarded, despite the fact that their teachings were little more than variations on the old gnostic heresies. For a more detailed accounting of those heresies, which incidentally form the underpinning of the New Age Movement and of Naziism, see my earlier book, *The Twisted Cross*.[28]

Monasteries and Convents during the Middle Ages were hotbeds of mysticism ... a fact that alternately won them the condemnation and approval of the Vatican as the various popes took over.

Helping The Oppressed

There is no doubt that persons who dabble in occultism will eventually become oppressed by their activity — and will need your help. Some victims will obviously need help and will seek it out. Others will obviously need help but won't seek it out because of either confusion or fear. Still others are currently happy in their occultism and cannot be helped — yet.

The first group is relatively easy to deal with because they already know they need something. The second group can be helped but only after they come to terms with their needs. Perhaps they need to have their fears diminished (which can include approaching Christians!) or their confusion sorted out. The third group cannot be helped until the oppressive nature of occultism is thrust upon them.

When occultists present themselves for assistance they may not believe that occultism is at the root of their problems. They have a history of seeming emotional or mental illness that either has no medical explanation or is intractible to medical intervention. The immediate problem may appear to be other than spiritual and may be diagnosible as one of the various forms of mental illness. But if the person has dabbled in occultism or if someone in past generations of their family was so involved, then suspect demonic oppression brought on by occultism. Frequently a sign pointing to occultism is the inability or unwillingness to confess Jesus as Christ — the *only* Christ.

It is tempting to turn afflicted occultists over to mental health professionals. Although this practice is what the standard wisdom of our culture may dictate, it is not the best procedure at all. In fact, intervention by the mental health establishment may actually make the condition worse. Except for that branch of psychiatry (which is practiced by medical doctors only) that deals with organically based mental illness, modern psychology is based on false premises (see Chapter 6).

For example, the secular psychologist rejects spiritual causes of illness altogether and his Christian counterpart is not far behind (having been seduced by the apparent "science" of psychology).

Besides rejection of the spiritual dimension, there is a more sinister reason for concern over psychology. Much of modern psychology, both Jungian and Freudian, has roots in the same poisoned well as the patient's illness: occultism. Using such psychology to fight the oppression of occultism is like filling the fireman's hose with gasoline instead of water.

The tactic to take in aiding the occultly oppressed depends upon whether the person is a believer. Although there is apparent warrant in scripture for the opinion that believers cannot be demon possessed, it is possible for the believer to be oppressed by demons. It is especially likely for a believer to be oppressed if he was involved in occultism, even innocently, before conversion. He can be oppressed to the extent that he did not renounce past practices or involvement.

Christian counseling uses scripture as the basis of authority. The basic premises of Christian counseling are that the person is a believer, accepts the authority of scripture and wants to please God. Christian counseling is very effective for persons who meet this criteria and somewhat ineffective for those who do not.

When the oppressed person is a believer it is appropriate to lead them to relevant scripture passages. There are many doctrines that are obscure enough that good people can honestly disagree over them: occultism is NOT one of them. God is very specific about human involvement in occultism and Deuteronomy 18:9-13 tells the complete story.

Listen to what the Word says:

> "...do not learn to imitate the detestable ways of the nations there [Canaan]. Let no one be found among you ... who practices divination or sorcery, interprets omens, engages in witchcraft or casts spells or who is a medium or spiritist or who consults with the dead."

The former occultist must confess sins of occultic involvement — all such participation must be confessed and given up. The person must renounce Satan and all his works and then command him to depart. Matthew 12:43-45 tells us that deliverance from demons is not an experience or an event but is a walk. It is essential, therefore, that the person counseling a former occultist takes steps to disciple them in the Christian life.

Occultists who have not become Christians cannot be helped until they are saved.[29] They must confess faith in Jesus Christ as Savior. If you encounter such a person, it is necessary first to get them to accept salvation and only then deal with their occultism. Be aware that some people seek relief from occultism and will confess Christ from the mouth rather than the heart. If relief doesn't seem to follow salvation over the next few months, then suspect that the conversion was not genuine and confront the person.

A Word For Occultists: The "Building Metaphor"

New Age spiritual teachers like to use metaphors to make their points. I would like to take a page or two from their notebook and use a metaphor of my own. Occultism can be represented by what I call the "Building Metaphor." The door to this building is very appealing and is quite innocent looking. The reception room is very attractively furnished: its colors are appealing and the furniture well designed. But beyond the entrance room the architecture seems a bit strange: it is a maze of crisscrossing corridors. Some are trails of truth but many are paths of error.

All of the passageways in the building eventually lead to a large inner chamber — where there is a chained tiger! Every now and then, as you travel the corridors of the occult, you will hear the distant roar of the tiger. An uneasy sense of dread envelopes your heart — but the sound seems so very far away, so you continue your Quest through that mystical maze.

We know that the tiger's chain is at least long enough to let him roam to all points of his room and anyone who treads into that dreadful space will be devoured. What we don't know, however, is how far up any given corridor the tiger can go. We also don't know when any given corridor will suddenly empty into that fatal inner room.

The wonderous corridors of the occult thrill the senses and excite the mind. Many new and heady experiences are to be had. Dozens of sights, sounds and feelings are found in those seductive spiritual corridors. There is wisdom to be had; ancient wisdom that (they tell you) is limited to a lucky few.

But you never know when turning a corner will bring you face-to-face with that tiger. You might be lucky — the tiger will spring with teeth bared and claws extended for the kill, only to be yanked up short by the chain, stopped in mid-jump; after all, God places some limits on the tiger.

You might not be so lucky. You may survive the attack but be clawed and seriously injured. Or, and this is a real possibility, you might also die in your occultism — and then it is too late for salvation. If you have not traveled too far or, if you are exceedingly lucky, then you may find the way back to the entrance room — and hopefully won't find the door locked!

Fortunately, there is a way out! Look up and you will find that the building has no roof. The walls are too slick to climb out by yourself but with the help of Jesus Christ you can be plucked out of that endless mystical maze.

Playing on the Streets of Babylon

The New Age Movement is the modern descendent of a centuries-long tradition of occultism that dates back to Babylon.[1] Although the Church from time to time tried to suppress the so-called "Ancient Wisdom," it nonetheless flourished alongside Christianity. It never went away, only underground and often not very far underground.

When theosophy married the Western Esoteric Tradition (occultism) to Eastern religions during the late 19th century, a natural resonance occurred that vibrates even today more than 100 years later. The Western Esoteric Tradition sometimes uses the metaphor of a scarlet serpent to describe itself. Christians recently found the tail of that serpent in the weeds alongside the road of Western civilization. Little did they realize as they yanked that tail that it was attached to a 20-foot King Cobra, rather than a harmless garter snake.

The New Age movement is not just opposed to Christianity but also orthodox Judaism. This fact persists in spite of the fact that many Jews are attracted to the movement. Orthodox and Conservative Jews accept the same basic concept of God as Christians (although they vehemently disagree with us on the other two persons of the Trinity), so would find the New Age concept of God a perverted heresy. Jews, whether or not they are religious, will ultimately find the New Age Movement (especially the Alice Bailey wing) anti-semitic right down to its esoteric core.

Bailey claimed in 1949 that Jews would have to go through the "fires of purification" before they could enter the New Age because of "bad racial karma" — a distinctly anti-semitic statement that was made only four years after the world was shocked by the crimes of the Holocaust![2] One New Age writer admitted in a book that Adolf Hitler was the movement's most famous proxy disciple.

New Age Theological Concepts

All religious movements have key theological concepts that either set them apart from or align them with other religions. In Christianity, for example, our theology tells us that God is personal, infinite, omnipotent and transcendent (that is, above and separate from His creation). There are only a few different views of God possible and they are ably presented in Dr. Norman Geisler's book *False Gods of Our Time* (Harvest House).[3] In this section, we will deal with only one of those possibilities: the New Age god-concept.

Pantheism The key New Age god-concept is "pantheism." This idea claims that all is God: I'm god, you're god, this book is god, the typewriter is god, etc. The pantheist's god is not personal but, rather, is a force, consciousness or essence in the universe. Some New Agers reduce God to a mere force of nature. "The Force" of *Star Wars* is a good example of a pantheistic god-concept.

Monism Monism, another key New Age idea, claims that everything is made ultimately of only one substance. Humans are said to be "One" with their race, with all of humanity, the planet, the solar system, indeed the entire universe. Differences are described as different facets of the same diamond. They claim that the planet, the solar system and the universe itself possesses a singular "Cosmic Consciousness" which is God (called "the One"). Pantheism and monism are almost always found linked in the same theory.[4]

A serious problem with the pantheistic/monistic world view is that it reduces God to a mere part of His own creation and thus removes the Infinite as a reference point for morals, ethics and values. By dismissing the absolute we fall into the bottomless pit of moral relativism. After all, who has the right to say that Hitler, Stalin and Mao Tse Tung were wrong to murder millions of people if there is no absolute? If All is One, then good is evil, evil is good and Adolf Hitler is interchangeable with yourself. Like Lucifer in Milton's *Paradise Lost,* we can boast "Evil, Be Thou Mine Good" without fear of either contradiction or divine rebuke.

Divinity of Man New Agers teach the ancient gnostic heresy that God made a terrible mistake at the Creation and managed to lock a bit of Himself in the "physical plane."[5] That part of God is said to be a spark of divinity inside each human soul. A main activity of New Agers is discovering, i.e, becoming conscious of, their supposed divinity; that search is called the "Quest" and the result is "self-realization."[6]

Altered States of Consciousness Part of the mystical Quest for many New Agers is achieving an altered state of consciousness through any of several psychospiritual technologies: drugs, yoga, meditation, Transcendental Meditation, biofeedback, creative visualization, guided imagery, positive imaging and so forth. Some New Age meditation techniques, which are yoga and not Christian, are nonetheless taught in churches as legitimate.

Books such as *Celebration of Discipline* by Richard J. Foster teach Eastern meditation, even while denying that it is Eastern.[7] Foster explicitly denies that his meditation is Eastern but then proceeds to introduce the reader to what seems uncomfortably like yogic meditation.

Inner Self The New Age teaches that God is within each of us and uses "Inner Self" as a name for God (or at least an ambiguous divinity). Thus, they claim that the Inner Self is always right and should be obeyed even when reason and external information indicates otherwise. This same idea is taught by several well-known Christians who would have us believe that the New Ager's "Inner Self" is the Holy Spirit. One radio preacher counseled obedience to the Inner Voice even when it seems to contradict Scripture; a very dangerous idea!

New Age Jargon

The New Age Movement uses a number of buzz-words and code phrases. Be suspicious when these phrases are found, even in a seemingly Christian context. Typical words are: Age of Aquarius, Cosmic Consciousness, Inner Self, enlightenment, Human Potential, illumination, holistic (and wholistic), at-ONE-ment, Positive Mental Attitude, paradigm shift, Confluent Education, Inner Healing, Healing of Memories, visualization, guided imagery, Global Village, transformation and so forth.

Be aware, however, that use of New Age buzz-words is not conclusive evidence of either involvement or guilt. While such word usage bears deeper investigation, it should not automatically condemn the user. The widespread familiarity with these words assures innocent as well as guilty usage. For example, I know a Bible college president who innocently used "global village" in a fund-raising letter. He is a

righteous and godly man whose missions zeal reso-
nated with the concept inherent in that New Age
phrase. Some critics, however, jump on such Christians and wrongly abuse them.

However, we must be wary of Christians who
couple terminology with doubtful practices that have
their origins in Eastern mysticism or Western occultism. Inner Healing is one such practice.[8] Inner Healing (or "Healing of Memories") proceeds from Jungian psychology (although the practitioners usually
deny it), which itself proceeds from occultism and
Carl Jung's "automatic writing" episode early in his
career (see Chapter 6).[9]

Luciferic Religion

The New Age Movement is openly Luciferic. One
does not have to read Lucifer into obscure passages
from minor writers because the leaders of the movement for more than 100 years have openly professed
Luciferianism. One New Age activity even once
called itself "Lucifer Publishing Company" (currently
Lucis Trust).[10] New Age Luciferians are not satanists
in the ordinary sense, however, for New Agers di-
vorce Lucifer from Satan! They teach that Lucifer is
the angel of man's evolution and a bridge to God.
They claim that he is merely the opposite aspect of Jesus but otherwise equal or superior to Jesus in every
respect. One New Age leader tells us "Lucifer has had
a bum rap from the church."

A major goal of the New Age is to force all humanity to take a "Luciferic Initiation" in order to enter the New Age alive under the auspices of one
World Religion. All people of the "old thought form"
(i.e., Christians, among others) who refuse the initiation will be zapped to another (non-physical) dimension when the New Age dawns (can you imagine a
better explanation for the Rapture?).

Constance Cumbey, author of *Hidden Dangers of the Rainbow*,[11] claims that the New Age is the first movement in history to meet all the scriptural tests of the antichrist Movement. Elliot Miller of Christian Research Institute has disagreed with Cumbey on some particulars. Yet in *Moody Monthly* Miller said: "... the 'Age of Aquarius' sounds uncomfortably close to the world pictured in Revelation 13-19, Matthew 24 and similar prophetic passages."[12]

The Great Delusion

Scripture paints a clear picture of conditions on earth at the end of the age, immediately prior to Christ's return. In a way, New Agers are correct when they postulate the coming of a new age for the Millenial (1000-year) reign of Jesus Christ on the earth will indeed be another, or new, age. Furthermore, that new age will be a time of universal peace, exactly as New Agers claim.

Where the Christian who understands end time prophecy differs with the New Ager, however, is the nature of the next age and the transition period between now and then. Sandwiched between the next age and this present one will be a brief period of intense barbarism called The Great Tribulation.[13]

Much has been written of end times in Christian literature. Some of these teachings are based solidly on scripture, while others are vain imagination. Much end times teaching is highly speculative and should not be taken as truth. Speculation is permissable, however, provided that it a) is plausible, b) does not contradict scripture and c) is accepted (and offered) as purely hypothetical.

Teachers who force-fit every bit of headline news into a prophetic mold do the Church a disservice. I can recall a Christian bookstore clerk who witnessed to a non-believer who wandered into the store.

She claimed: "Do you know that the Bible teaches we will all be required to have a laser credit card surgically implanted in the palm of our hands?" The Bible teaches no such thing! Nor does it teach that a computer chip will be embedded in our hands or any of a number of other variations on the "666" theme favored by prophecy buffs on the fringe. Such things may honorably be speculated about and may indeed eventually turn out to be true. But we must keep our speculation properly labelled as speculation and not pass it off as scriptural.

Studying the rise of antichrist leads many to the conclusion that this final movement of Satan will be primarily political. It is true that politics will play a role for it is in politics that we find the mechanism of domination. But most such commentators miss a critical point: the activity of antichrist is primarily *religious* in nature. To overemphasize the political at the expense of the religious is the same as overlooking Jesus in favor of the donkey he used to ride into Jerusalem.

In this section we will examine the religious aspects of the antichrist movement.

There are two aspects to the antichrist religion: apostasy and false religions. The word "apostasy" means "a falling away from the faith." What is our basis for believing that a great apostasy will occur?

The answer is found in I Timothy 4:1-3:

> "The spirit clearly says in later times some will abandon the faith and follow deceiving spirits and things taught by demons. Such teachings come through hypocritical liars"[NIV].

This passage tells us three things.

First, apostasy will occur ("...some will abandon the faith"). Evidence is all around us that this falling away is happening. So many have fallen away from the faith that both theologian Francis Schaeffer and humanist writers call our era "post-Christian" (on that single issue the humanists are likely to agree with Dr. Schaeffer!).[14] In addition, Christian teachers who have been conservative and orthodox in their theology have publicly endorsed heretic teachings.

Second, we learn that the source of the apostate teachings is ultimately "deceiving spirits" and demons.

Finally, that the apostate teachers are hypocritical liars. For the words "hypocritical" and "liars" to apply, assumes that the false teachers *know the truth but teach otherwise!*

When we see seemingly large numbers of teachers in pulpits, on radio and TV and in our colleges teaching doctrines and practices that strain orthodoxy to the snapping point, we must conclude that this prophecy is coming true. Although one is tempted to simply blast the heretics in outrage, Paul tells us why these men and women are successful (I Timothy 4:3,4):

> "For the time will come when men will not put up with sound doctrine. Instead, to suit their own desires, they will gather around them a great number of teachers to say what their itching ears want to hear. They will turn their ears away from the truth and turn aside to myths"[NIV].

Three things present themselves in this passage. One striking characteristic of our age is that men will not only turn away from sound, Bible-based doctrine but will become intolerant of it. Doesn't that sound like today? And what will men use to replace sound doctrine? The words of false teachers who say what their itching ears want to hear.

How are we to understand this teaching of Paul? The remedy is the same for all false teachings: exposure, rebuttal and exposition of the biblically correct doctrinal position. We must be especially wary of apostasy that links arms with a false religion: the New Age Movement.

Although the specifics differ from that of apostate Christians, New Agers nonetheless share in the Great Delusion. Again, scripture predicts much of what we see in the Movement today. After all, the New Age religion is nothing more than a modern variant of the ancient Babylonian mystery religion; somewhat changed and disguised but nonetheless the same old lie.

Second Thessalonians 2:11-12 reveals that God, because they have refused to love the truth, " ... and delight in wickedness," has sent them "a powerful delusion." It takes only a cursory examination of the word "delusion" to see that people will adhere to something that seems right but is not. Such a description fits the New Age exactly for its adherants believe they have found the truth, where in fact they have found a seemingly rational lie.

A mark of the Great Delusion in the end time is the appearance of multiple fake candidates for the office of "Christ."

Witness Matthew 24:3-5:

> "... and what will be the sign of your coming and of the end of the age?" Jesus answered: "Watch out that no one deceives you. For many will come in my name, claiming, 'I am the Christ,' and will deceive many."

From this passage it is apparent that on the cusp between this age and the Millenium, we will be beseiged with false christs. In Matthew 24:24-25 we see a prediction that should give pause for concern to those who believe that performing miracles is evidence of the Holy Spirit:

"For false christs and false prophets will appear and perform great signs and miracles ... ."

Most Christians seem unaware that miracles abound among New Agers. In fact, the question is not whether occultism works but rather how well it works. The world-famous Findhorn garden in Scotland, for example, produced 40-pound cabbages in the cold, flinty North Sea region where little else of anything grows at all.[15] And what was the source of such miracles? The Holy Spirit? No, "nature spirits."

Reading New Age literature leads one very quickly to the conclusion that it is Luciferic. How fitting and how indicative of end-times happenings! Yet it comes at a time when much of the church has either neglected Lucifer, chooses to ignore Lucifer or reduces him to the absurdity of a comical goat-headed creature. But we need not depend upon Lucifer being repulsive or ugly. People would never follow the goat-headed, hoofed Devil of the Middle Ages.

Lucifer is not like that — he is an angel of light and God's most beautiful creation. When people encounter such a lovely being doing miraculous things, they are likely to be deceived. Yet, make no mistake about it — he is still Lucifer, the Devil and is the ultimate evil.

Christians In The New Age
The New Age Movement attracts not just spiritually concerned non-Christians but Christians as well. Most of these people are ignorant of their involvement in the New Age heresy. Many social and political goals of the New Age Movement are very attractive to people who are concerned over the suffering of others. But Globalism, for example, is still a New Age concept, even when proposed by Christians.

In other cases, New Age ideas infiltrate the church

and appear under Christian imprimature. Many writers on life after death (or "near death") experiences are actually promoting a New Age concept and some of them admit it, even while still claiming to be Christian.

Some writers are now pushing meditation. Christian meditation is an intense intellectual activity and is defined as "pondering deeply God's Word." It is a matter of using the intellect that God gave us to discern the meaning of scriptures. It is not an emptying of the mind to make room for the closeness with God being sought by the mystical meditator. When we empty our mind through meditative techniques, we are in essence abandoning the driver's seat and inviting a demon to take control.

In the meditation of the New Age, emptying the mind is exactly what is sought. They will use one technique or another to "center down" into the meditative trance. *Celebration of Discipline* teaches a New Age concept of meditation.[16] Its author, Richard J. Foster, even affirms the connection on page 170 with the statement: "We of the New Age ... " In later printings of the book, this revealing phrase was changed to, "We who follow Christ ... " As far as I can tell, however, this is the only alteration of the book, so it remains a New Age book in my opinion.

Foster's chapter on meditation contains a scenario that sounds a lot like accounts of astral projection I have heard elsewhere. Foster makes the claim that his method is different from Eastern meditation. Eastern meditation leads to emptying the mind, while Foster's meditation leads to emptying the mind so that it can be filled again. My problem with Foster's claim is that I am concerned over who and what does the filling; how do we know it is the Holy Spirit at work? For these reasons, I believe that Richard Foster's books need to be approached with utmost caution, even though he probably believes himself an orthodox Christian and is probably bewildered at his critics' charges.

One New Age writer tells us that it doesn't matter which path is followed to attain the trance because, once they get to the meditation stage all experiences are the same. This is the principal danger of both New Age meditation and so-called "Christian" meditation. The meditation of the Christian is functionally different from the meditation of the New Age: the Christian asks God to show him the way *intellectually* through pondering scripture, the New Ager lets a ghost operate his or her brain.

Taking Dominion In The New Age

A new fad movement is sweeping the church, and is especially strong amongst Pentecostals and Charismatics.[17] This movement blends some of the New Age Movement's Eastern religious ideas with several variants of either Postmillenialism or Amillenialism (both long-since discredited) to form a sticky, cookie-dough, hybrid doctrine that harks back to Eden. Like a too-sweet cookie, this doctrine offers little nutrition, but nonetheless rots your spiritual teeth. Because it is so dangerous spiritually, it is necessary that we discuss it.

A leading exponent of this "Kingdom Now" or "Dominion" theology movement wrote:[18]

"Adam and Eve were placed as the seed and expression of God. Just as dogs have puppies and cats have kittens, so God has little gods. Seed remains true to its nature, bearing its own kind.

"When God said, 'let us make man in our image,' He created us as little gods, but we have trouble comprehending this truth."[19]

In this passage, the writer lays nearly the same divinity of man foundation as the New Age Movement and makes exactly the same mistake as Eve in the Garden of Eden. When Dave Hunt, Constance Cumbey, Jimmy Swaggart and others critized him for these views, the author apparently backpeddled and claimed that he was only kidding. He made this claim on October 16, 1986 in a speech given at the Westpark Hotel in Tyson's Corners, Virginia (suburban Washington, D.C.).[20]

He also stated at that same meeting that anyone who thinks that we are gods is sick. Yet the quote above is taken in all seriousness by readers of his book, and one can only assume that he meant it when he wrote it. After all, very few healthy writers waste energy telling little jests that don't work in print. The quotes in his book don't appear in jest when its context is evaluated.

A key element in the Dominion teaching is that God either will not, or cannot, perform total restoration of the paradise of Eden until Christians take dominion over the earth. They erroneously appeal to II Thessalonians in claiming that Christ cannot return until there is a "... falling away of those Christians who are unwilling to endure to the end." [21]

Yet scripture tells us that Christ will return after the rebellion against God, and the Man of Lawlessnes (antichrist) is revealed. The great falling away revealed in scripture is the great delusion discussed above. Second Thessalonians admonishes us to stand firm to the end, not in dominion over the earth, but in "... the teachings we passed on to you ..." As to antichrist, these people claim that antichrist is only a spirit, and doesn't refer to an actual man.

Although Dominionists claim to esteem doctrinal orthodoxy, they nonetheless hold that scripture, God's revealed Word, is insufficient for today. Some things, they maintain, would have been unlawful to reveal to man in the past because of his spiritual immaturity (which is like the New Age concept of mystical Initiation). But now, because of (presumedly Dominionist) man's maturity, new revelations can be offered. One exponent teaches that scripture is but milk for babes. And what is the meat to nurture the more spiritually mature? It is new revelation and direct experiential religion. Direct experiential religion is part and parcel of the ancient gnostic heresy, and is also the mainstay of New Age spiritual life. Yet a man who is, perhaps, the leading Dominionist ridiculed the claim that his ideas are New Age.[22]

Perhaps the most disturbing part of Dominionist teaching is that God has put the Tree of Life and the Tree of Knowledge of Good and Evil in the church today. Scripture clearly tells us otherwise, and yet these heretics want us to believe that God has reversed Himself since Eden. Are they right? Or have the Dominionists taken a very deep, second bite of the apple?

Because of the frequent and very obvious gross errors in interpreting scripture, one can only conclude that Dominionists deny that scripture is to be taken literally. In reading several Dominionists, I can only conclude that the errors are intentional. One prominent Dominionist ridiculed Dave Hunt as a man who has not attended even a day of bible school, yet his own position denies the validity of scripture for the modern church.

Sad.

David Lewis, a leading Pentecostal who has campaigned against the Dominion/Kingdom-Now heresy, and Constance Cumbey, author of *Hidden Dangers of the Rainbow,* have both written that a New Age leader boasted that New Age thinking had invaded Neo-Pentecostalism. According to Cumbey, writing in her controversial second book, *A Planned Deception:*

The Staging of a New Age Messiah, Ernest Ramsey was "Already familiar with the Alice Bailey writings, [and] he was amazed to see that there was a branch of Pentecostalism that embraced the same teachings ...."

Other Dominionists harp on economics instead of theology. A certain wing of that movement has obviously overdosed on the writings of philosopher Ayn Rand, and even mimmick her style by using similar phraseology (in one case, almost to the point of intellectual plagiarism, if not in the legal sense of the word). I find that fact particularly amusing because I am familiar with (and have since rejected many of) the works of Rand. Ayn Rand, the apparent heroine of certain Dominionists, an avowed atheist, claimed that atheism was necessary to her philosophy and despised American conservatives whose politics are like those of the Dominionists.

(I met my wife at an Ayn Rand study group in college; that was before being saved. We like to startle people by telling them we met in an atheist study group.)

Dominionists tell us that Christ admonished us "... to occupy until He comes." One enthusiastically jumps off a semantic cliff by claiming:

"The word 'occupy' is a military word for occupational force. An occupational force is a group of soldiers who slip behind the enemy's line, grab a piece of his territory, and claim it and hold it until the invasion comes."

Dominionists must disdain dictionaries. Such a force might be a commando unit, but it is not an occupational force. An occupational force moves into enemy territory and takes over civil government ... *after the final victory*. The Dominionist claim apparently refers to Luke 19:13. In this passage we find Jesus giving his followers a parable. In Luke 19:11 we find that the parable was offered to them because they erroneously believed "... that the kingdom of God should immediately appear." Jesus' parable was of a nobleman who went to a far country to recieve for himself a kingdom, and returned. In the subject verse, Luke 19:13, we find the nobleman gave each of his 10 servants a sum of money and told them "... Occupy till I come" [KJV].

How is this to be understood? According to the Dominionists this apparently means that Christians are to militarily occupy earth, and hold it until Jesus returns. Relying on translations in more modern English than the King James, we find a slightly different coloration. *The New International Version* (NIV) renders Luke 19:13 as follows:

> *"And he called ten of his slaves, and gave them ten minas, and said to them, 'Do business with this until I come back.' "*

Similarly, the *New American Standard Bible* [NASB] renders the passage:

> *"So he called ten of his servants and gave them ten minas. 'Put this money to work,' he said, 'until I come back.' "*

These translations put in doubt the Dominionist interpretation.

How to React to the New Age

How should the New Age Movement affect us? We must not react hysterically for one thing. Although we need to be alert, we should not worry overmuch about it. Some pastors and lay leaders go to the opposite extreme, however, claiming that we should pay no attention at all to the New Age Movement. They ask "why pay heed to such negative, evil things?" The best reason is that the New Age Movement robs people of genuine salvation by offering them a counterfeit. New Age questors drink not from the living waters of the true well of life but rather from a well whose waters are eternally poisoned. If for no other reason than that, Christians must contend with the New Age Movement!

Whether the New Age Movement is the antichrist movement spoken of in prophecy is not terribly important to the church, even though it is of vital importance to nonbelievers. We, after all, are saved and they are not. What is important is that it is a movement that steals salvation through polluted doctrines. For that reason, Christians ought to oppose the New Age.

Until the late 19th century there was a much deeper level of secrecy enshrouding the movement. New Agers will tell you that the Hierarchy started the process of Externalizing in 1875 with the revelations given to Madame Blavatsky and other early theosophists. The Externalization of the "Hierachy" got underway, according to certain New Agers, with the Occult Revival. For the past 100 years, about the same time the church has been internalizing, the New Age Movement has been making the esoteric movement exoteric.

Starting in 1975 or thereabouts, the movement "went public."[24] Fueled by an influx of mystically inclined young people armed with their recent drug experiences, the Movement became far more open than before. Today, the New Age Movement is almost totally open. Every city and town of any size has its own New Age centers and activities; many of them have one or more New Age newspapers. The probability of Christians who work in secular jobs encountering at least one New Ager every month is close to 100 percent.

Perhaps the reason that many Christians fail to see the Movement is that it is still novel. They erroneously assume that it is a minor ripple on the pond of American civilization and, like other transient movements, it will go away. But it will not simply go away; wax and wane, maybe, but not go away. After all, it already has a multi-millenia track record.

Even Christians who see the Movement clearly often fail to grasp its extent. When Constance Cumbey, Dave Hunt, Johanna Michelson, the Matricianos[25] and others spoke of an immense and widespread movement they were dismissed as overstating their case. Yet New Age directories list thousands of organizations! The widespread activity of the New Age becomes readily apparent when a systematic study is made and it is now possible to call it the fastest growing and possibly the largest, new religion on earth.

Perhaps the best church reaction to both the New Age and the heresies within our own ranks is to heed Paul's charge to Timothy:

> *"But you, keep your head in all situations, endure hardships, do the work of an **evangelist**, discharge all the duties of your ministry"* [II Timothy 4:5].

Visualization:

Christian or Occultic?

You are seated with a group of people in a small room. Your eyes are closed and your breathing is measured.

"Close your eyes and relax," suggests the group leader in a soft, comforting voice; "imagine that you are going to a warm, cozy, place far away ... from a long distance you see a figure approaching. He is too far away to tell who it is at first but as the figure comes closer the vision is clearer. He is your spirit guide ... imagine that he is Jesus."[1]

The process described above is is one of several related mystical New Age techniques that are called "visualization" (among other names). Over the past two decades these methods rapidly became popular among psychologists, holistic healers, physicians, nurses and others. Visualization swept through the church during the last several years and is now very popular in some Christian groups, especially Charismatics and Pentecostals. It is billed as a technique for losing weight, quitting smoking, obtaining "Inner Healing," achieving a deeper spirituality and even a closer walk with Christ.

Visualization is a favorite technique of Christians who accept the "Faith, Health and Prosperity" teachings. They use it as a means for obtaining the material benefits that they claim is God's will for all of us. For many of the same reasons, secular sales organizations use visualization to motivate sales people: "put a picture of that Cadillac where you can see it, close your eyes and just imagine yourself owning that car!" screams frenzied speakers at high tension motivational meetings.

The purpose of visualization is to put our rational minds in neutral so that images can stream forth, supposedly from deep within. We are asked to enter an altered state of consciousness about which we know very little, except that it is shamanic. Although initial attempts at visualization rarely achieve the desired result, with practice the visualizer soon learns to enter a state of consciousness that bears more than a superficial resemblance to hypnosis and the mystical shamanic trances generated by hyperventilation, ecstatic dance, self-flagellation, drugs, yogic meditation and others.[2]

Ordinarily, our spirit controls the firing of the neurons in our brains. But in an altered state, that control mechanism is loosened and it becomes possible for other spirits to tick off those neurons. The critical question "which spirits?" is rarely asked by casual visualizers.

Although touted as a "higher consciousness," visualization and other popular psychospiritual techniques may instead result in lowered consciousness. That is, as we loosen conscious bounds on our imagination, we are open to whatever thoughts uncritically enter our brain. Our normal powers of rational discernment are put aside in an altered state of consciousness, so sensory inputs tend to melt together. Although taken as evidence of the oneness of all creation, it may instead be true that this effect results from an inability to critically focus the mind — which causes the victim to perceive counterfeit unity. If normal consciousness implies control over our minds — the God-given, rational faculty needed to discern reality and truth — then surrendering control moves us to a lower, not higher, state of consciousness.

Visualization is offered as a near cure-all for a variety of spiritual, psychological, physical and economic ills. It is widely accepted by Christians but is it either biblical or at least neutral? In fact, is it even safe? Is it the Holy Spirit who guides your visualized imagery or are you opening your mind to demonic influence? These and other critical questions need answers before visualization is accepted by Christians.

Christian Visualization

Visualization is now very popular among Christians and books recommending it are on the bestseller list.[3] A major Charismatic television ministry uses visualization in its pastoral outreach arm. I once heard a pastor on TV mimmick the sales motivator by claiming that we should ask God for a Cadillac, believe that we already have it (a key to visualization success), see it in our mind's eye (in other words, visualize it) and then it will somehow be delivered. Perhaps he should have said "manifested" (New Age) or "materialized" (witchcraft) instead of "delivered."

Besides being firmly rooted in both classical Western occultism and Eastern mysticism, such methods force God into the role of a cosmic Aladdin's lamp, a god of convenience or spiritual vending machine: Since when does the sovereign God do our bidding on command? No matter how these teachings are dressed up, they bear the stigma of demeaning the unspeakable majesty of God!

It is apparent that much of this type of activity is little more than sorcery.[4] That's a big claim, so let's put it to rest by considering the definition of sorcery. As we explained earlier, the two words translated "sorcery" in Scripture are *magia* and *pharmakaea.* The latter is the root of "pharmacy" and probably refers to the seeking of mystical experiences or supernatural powers through the use of consciousness altering drugs. Some American indian tribes legally use peyote (mescaline) for this purpose in their religious rituals.

The other word, *magia,* refers to ritual magic, which can be defined as:

> *"The attempt to influence or control the natural or supernatural worlds through supernatural beings, laws, energies, forces or entities by means of words, practices or rituals that in and of themselves have power."*[5]

— spirits

Keep in mind that we are not talking about genuine prayer but rather about words (etc.) *that in and of themselves have power* that is released regardless of who uses them ... or when.[6] Clearly, if the visualizer is attempting to create health, wealth or material goods out of thin air through the practice of visualization, then he or she is conducting a shaman's or sorcerer's ritual. Visualization is a key part of the ritual.

Occultic Visualization

Visualization is a New Age technique and, as such, it is taught in many New Age seminars, personal transformation courses and in numerous New Age books (some of which are sold in Christian bookstores). Even the medical profession has fallen for this bit of quackery. Nurses and nursing administrators in hospitals all over the country attend seminars and retreats that feature visualization, meditation and other forms of concealed sorcery.

A handout given to head nurses in one community hospital proclaimed that the nurse could become a magician. Although the nurses who attended the seminar took it metaphorically, the real intent was apparently a lot closer to the plain-sense meaning of the words selected: *they want to make nurses into shamanic magicians!*[7]

Visualization is a spiritual exercise that is defined by New Agers as " ... using your imagination to create what you want in life." You can supposedly use visualization to gain wealth, power, material goods, health, healing and spiritual guidance. But, claim its fans, it is not necessary to "have faith" in anything external to yourself.

Visualization is thus said to be completely natural; merely a suppressed ability of primal man; perhaps something that Adam and Eve lost at the garden gate. Most New Age occultists call these techniques "Creative Visualization" or "Guided Imagery." It is also sometimes called "Dynamic Imaging," "Positive Imaging" or simply "Visualization;" but we should call it "Occultic Visualization" to keep it in proper spiritual perspective.

Even though faith in something supernatural is not required, the same New Agers tell us "it helps" and the trust we are asked to place in the "spirit guide" whom we visualize sounds a lot like religious faith. A leading New Age writer on this topic, Shakti Gawain (author of *Creative Visualization*), tells us it is " ... magic in the highest meaning of the word."[8] Its magical aspect is supported by its inclusion in *The Magic Power of Witchcraft* by Gavin and Yvonne Frost (Gavin Frost is Archbishop of the church of Wicca).[9]

Shamanism In The Church?

Visualization is also a tool in the kit of the primitive shaman.[10] Although scoffed at by Westerners as mere "medicine men" or "witch doctors," they are nonetheless widely respected in primitive cultures for their ability to contact the spirit world. If these aboriginal mystics were merely fraudulent, then their hold over the people would vanish in a pile of repeated failures. Only our educated haughtiness assumes that primitive peoples are too ignorant to recognize fraudulent shaman.

That shamans use visualization is well documented by Dr. Michael Harner and others. According to Harner, an anthropologist and himself a practicing shaman, there are two states of consciousness: the ordinary state of consciousness (OSC) and the shamanic state of consciousness (SSC). In his book *The Way of the Shaman*, Harner tells us that when a shaman enters the SSC he " ... become(s) a seer and undertake(s) personally the famed shamanic journey to acquire firsthand knowledge of a hidden universe" (p.xix). Although primitive shamans speak of meeting spirits — testimonies that sound startlingly like those we heard from westerners on LSD trips only a generation ago — Doctor Harner downplays the existence of these beings (p. xxi).

In the Afterword of his book (p.175), Harner reveals deep insight into modern New Age practices:

> *The burgeoning field of holistic medicine shows a tremendous amount of experimentation involving the reinvention of many techniques long practiced in shamanism, such as visualization, altered state of consciousness, aspects of psychoanalysis, hypnotherapy, meditation, positive attitude, stress-reduction and mental and emotional expression of personal will for health and healing* [Emphasis added].[11]

In other words, Christians who practice visualization are in effect practicing forbidden shamanism regardless of their personal popularity, apparent success with miracle healings or their financially well-endowed ministry.

What's Wrong With Visualization?

Visualization techniques are very popular among self-improvement teachers in seemingly non-religious settings. They will tell you that visualization can help you lose weight, stop smoking or overcome almost any personal problem. There is ample evidence that visualization actually works. The testimony of visualizers from primitive shamans to modern New Agers is proof.[12]

So what's wrong with visualization? Why can't we visualize Jesus? Why can't we use the technique to obtain material wealth, physical health, "inner healing" and other benefits? After all, if Norman Vincent Peale, Agnes Sanford, Richard Foster and other Christian leaders teach the method, can it be all that bad? *Yes it can!*

First, no one knows what Jesus looks like. Virtually everyone will have a different Jesus and that's confusion where the real Jesus is never in confusion. Furthermore, the vision is not Jesus, only a representation.

A.W. Tozer teaches us that people who imagine God wind up with an imaginary god. Writing in *That Incredible Christian*, Tozer warns us "true faith is not the intellectual ability to visualize unseen things to the satisfaction of our minds, it is rather the moral power to trust Christ."[13]. From the same source we also learn from Tozer: "The wise Christian will not let his assurance depend upon his powers of imagination."[14].

We must recognize that Satan is an "angel of light" who can lead us to mistake a visualized counterfeit for the real Jesus. Those who trust their visualized "Jesus" because he seems so real argue that a counterfeit must closely mimmick the genuine to be accepted. They argue that there must be real gold before "fool's gold" makes sense. This argument is false and is nothing more than a stolen concept. By asserting that counterfeit visualization exists, we implicitly accept the premise that some visualization is genuinely of God. Thus, we tacitly accept that our own visualization experiences are genuine, while those of others are suspect. The end result is delusion.

Perhaps the reason why Jesus left no snapshots of himself — and the reason for the "no graven images" command given to the Hebrews — was that man will make the mere image into a god — an idol — and fall away from genuine worship. A "visualized Jesus" is only an idol made of thoughts. When found in the church, according to Dave Hunt, it is "evangelical idolotry."

Johanna Michaelson, author of *The Beautiful Side of Evil*, is a former New Ager who became a Christian. During her New Age time she was an assistant to a psychic surgeon (a witch named "Pachita") in Mexico City.[15] She reports in her book that she learned visualization through a Silva Mind Control course.[16] She was taught to create a "laboratory" in her mind where her guides could come and visit. Instead of seeing them a long way off she would instead wait for the lab door to open to reveal her guides. Being from a Christian culture, Johanna chose "Jesus" as one of her guides. The first time he came, the visualized "Jesus" was quite conventional. The second time he visited her, however, he was in the form of a blood drenched werewolf! The lesson that she was apparently meant to learn was to not fear something that appeared evil; how convenient for Satan.

There is still another problem with visualization. The visualizer is often told to "see" Jesus any way he likes, in blue jeans and T-shirt for example. To visualize Jesus in an unworthy way is to allow ourselves to degrade the Holy God who is majesty unspeakable to a point that is simply sacrilegious. One proponent of visualization uses the example of famous artists who depicted Jesus in their paintings as justification for the practice.[17] There is a fundamental difference between artists and visualizers, however: those artists were working from intellect out of awe and respect. They were in complete possession of their mental faculties. But what visualizers recommend sounds too much like shamanistic self-hypnosis to be trusted! Furthermore, Christian artists through the ages have portrayed either the passion of Jesus or a glorified Jesus — not a hippie ragamuffin or a werewolf.

Finally, we lose our rational judgement to the extent that we soon learn to trust our spirit guides. Visualizers report that the bond formed with the guide is very tight.[18] The visualizer thus comes to implicitly trust everything that the guide says. For example, temptation could be less easily resisted when the spirit guide states that adultery is not adultery in your specific situation.

Other opinions can also be distorted. For example, you might come to believe that abortion on demand is clearly God's will for some people and not for others. A wicked man perceived as innocent could be elected to high political office by the votes of visualizers whose guides told them that he is God's choice for the office. Depending upon your favorite end times scenario, it is therefore easy to see how the antichrist might be a future European prime minister or United States president — elected by the faithful who were duped by their spirit guides.

Can We "Test The Spirits?"

Don't be misled by those who advise you to go ahead with visualization but to "test the spirits" against the Word of God along the way. That advice is a comfortable cop-out that can lead you astray. There are at least two problems with such advice.

First, the advice will soon go unheeded. William James, writing in *The Varieties of Religious Experience*, calls mystical experiences "ineffable." That is, mystical experiences are so beautiful that they are beyond the power of words to express. Thus, the visualizer will be overcome with wonderment and awe, so will soon put the advice aside and trust the "guide" completely.

A warm, fuzzy feeling of intense spirituality is no substitute for hardheaded testing in Scripture. Hard-nosed flicking off of your mental television set is the answer. After all, why intentionally expose yourself to spirits that need testing when you have the Word? Why did Paul commend the Bereans? Was it for testing everything by Scripture or for tripping off into the high, lonesome, thin upper atmosphere of mysticism?

Second, God may not protect you while visualizing. If visualization is witchcraft, sorcery or magick, then by practicing it you would be in a state of disobedience (Deut. 18:9ff). God will forgive visualizers on an eternal scale, as promised but He may nonetheless allow them to suffer the consequences of their disobedience on the temporal scale. After all, those who leap from the pinnacle of the temple still (to their chagrin) have to answer to the law of gravity; so it also is for other sins of presumption.

Visualization lets a spirit run a video tape inside your brain — and that spirit could be a deceiving demon. Sir John Eccles' statement, "the brain is a machine a ghost can operate," takes on hideous new meaning. The experiences reported by many visualizers shows that you cannot control either the content or who runs that mental peep show!

In Deuteronomy 18 God forbids trafficking with

spirits, witchcraft and other kindred things and for good reason. Such mystical experiences can be deceivingly beautiful (witness Michaelson's book title). You will come to trust your visualized "Jesus" so much that he can plant doctrinal errors in your mind by "explaining" or "clarifying" Scripture or by granting supposedly new revelations. You will then doubt your pastors, elders, teachers and even the Bible itself. You can also be led into erroneous political or social opinions (and actions) by your demonic "guide."

Why has Satan thrust visualization onto both the church and the New Age Movement at the same time? With New Agers, Christians, Jews, Hindus and Moslems all awaiting a messiah, the antichrist will gain quicker acceptance if millions of spiritually oriented people are told by their visualized guides that antichrist is their longed-for Jesus, Messiah, Imam Mahdi, Buddha or Lord Maitreya. Can the "Elect" be deceived? It would seem so — at least temporarily.

Not one word of scripture advocates or even hints at the practice of visualization, so it is therefore at least a suspect thing. Historically, visualization has not been found among Christians except for the monastic mystics of old, many of whom were excommunicated for heresy. Yet visualization is widely found among primitive and classical pagans, especially those with shamanistic religious systems. The practice is also found extensively among modern New Agers, as a quick visit to almost any New Age bookstore will reveal.

Nevertheless, many people in the church practice and teach visualization. When confronted with the facts about visualization, they become very defensive and usually attack the one criticizing the practice.

Dave Hunt, author of *The Seduction of Christianity*,

has been reviled by Christians who accept visualization and other occultic techniques. In defending their own involvement with the occult, Hunt's critics claim that he "throws out the baby with the bath water;" implying that there might be a clean Christian baby in all that dirty occultic bathwater. Hunt answered those critics in a video tape series by asserting that he searched for that baby in the bathwater and found it: *it was Rosemary's baby.*

We would do well to avoid visualization on grounds that it is:

• not scripturally authorized,

• practiced widely among non-Christian religions,

• a well-known practice of witchcraft, shamanism and sorcery and

• therefore strictly forbidden by God (Deuteronomy 18:9-18 and others).

We must conclude that visualization, whether in Christian churches or the local witchcraft/New Age meeting, is occultic. As such, visualization is condemned in Deuteronomy 18 and elsewhere in scripture.

Modern Psychology:

Renaming the Old Demons?

Perhaps never before did man plumb so deeply the depths of his own being as in the modern semi-science of psychology. The work of the early pioneers of psychology, intellectual giants like Sigmund Freud and Carl Gustav Jung, laid the foundation for all modern work in the field.

Until very recently, however, when neurological scientists, physiological psychologists and brain chemistry researchers became reputable, psychology's legitimate claim to being "science" was flimsy. At best it was a soft science and more art than science in clinical settings. Even in secular universities the psychologists sometimes endure the snickers of their faculty colleagues in the physical and life sciences departments.

It is axiomatic that a field that offers a large number of different answers to the same set of problems doesn't have any good answers; psychology is a field with too many answers. While no one would deny that Jung and Freud were intellectual giants or claim that they and their successors made no useful contributions, it is necessary to examine their underlying world views to see if the founding premises of psychology are valid. After all, if a system of thought is built on false premises or a faulty world view, then that system is like a house built on a foundation of sand.

Both Jung and Freud came of age intellectually in Europe during the height of the Occult Revival. This well-documented upsurge in occultism started in the 1840s with the Fox sisters and their Spiritualism but dates back millenia in the form of the Western Esoteric Tradition. In 1875, the theosophists of Madame Helena Petrovna Blavatsky blended together into one occultic system three streams of thought: the Western Esoteric Tradition, Eastern religions and Darwinian science. This new system flourished and is now called the New Age Movement. In an even more perverted form it became Naziism. My book, *The Twisted Cross,* describes the New Age occultism of Hitler.

The rise of science and materialism stripped away man's immortality but left him with nothing in return. Man became, in the materialist view, little more than a slurry of chemical elements and electrical currents choreographed in some sort of physical concert.

The freedom that we value so highly today was disorienting to many 19th-century men; to them, strong central authority meant not oppression but order.

Traditional secular governments lost their authority in the century of revolution from 1775 to 1875. The church also lost much of its authority. It lost some authority to the scientists and voluntarily gave up the rest to liberal Higher Criticism theology; God, if any, was declared dead.

The prospect of total extinction rightly terrified men who no longer had confidence in Christ for their salvation. Many of them could not accept either the materialist or the Christian world views, so turned instead to the occultism that was always present as a hidden underground stream in European culture from the earliest pre-Christian times.

At the turn of the century, when the Occult Revival was at its peak, Freud and Jung were studying the nature of man's mind. Yet even a casual reading of the Jungian and Freudian literature reveals that both men had mystical/occultic world views blended uncomfortably with the materialist world view that was then prevalent in science. It must have been a confusing time!

Materialism was one of the principal forces to emerge from the 19th century. This view was derived from the Age of Reason and the Enlightenment of earlier centuries and the rise of respectable science in the 19th century. Prior to Newton, Maxwell, Darwin and other giants of science, the track record of scientists allowed only amused skepticism. But by the 19th century science achieved the status of omnipotent wisdom; scientists could do no wrong and, in the popular mind, replaced the priests of earlier ages. No longer were scientists merely secular heretics in a hostile religious world.

The fathers of psychology joined other scientists in promoting the materialist world view. But there were conflicts: both Freud and Jung flirted with occultism and metaphysics and Jung never gave it up; it is debatable whether Freud ever gave it up completely (some say he merely renamed the same old demons).[1]

Carl Jung is rightly regarded by Neo-gnostics as the High Priest of their movement. Even in his time Jung was called the *Hexenmeister* ("warlock" or male witch) of Zurich. According to James Webb in *The Occult Establishment*: "Jung's psychology represents to many a restatement of the ideas at the core of occult tradition in terms accessible to those ill at ease with religious language. The point can be most strongly made by examining the way in which Jung was inspired to compare the stages in the 'alchemical process' with those he observed during the course of his patients' 'individuation.'"[2]

Another authority, Stephan Hoeller (director of the Sophia gnostic Center in Los Angeles and author of *The Gnostic Jung*) quotes a former associate[3]: "Dr. Jung is a seer and a mystic after the fashion of the magicians of the Renaissance. I have known for some time that there is more to him than meets the academic eye. Unlike Freud, he is not fearful of the dark mysteries of the spirit."[4]

Dr. Jung delved into gnosticism and alchemy and, indeed, saw alchemy as the bridge between ancient gnosticism and modern psychology. Alchemy he judged to be a modern pansophistic expression of gnosticism, Hermetic Neo-Platonism and other ancient esoteric traditions. To Jung, gnosticism was " ... not a set of doctrines but a mythological expression of an inner experience," and that same inner experience was the theme of his psychological theories. The images of the *gnosis* valued by the mystics were analogous to the "Archetypes" of Jungian psychology. According to Webb: "the plain result is that psychoanalysis, psychical research and the more religious aspects of the Occult Revival can by no means be disentangled."[5]

The evidence is strong that Doctor Jung was "... subject to paranormal experiences; and these naturally played a great part in orienting his system."[6] He experienced psychic visions throughout his childhood and even spoke of a mysterious event regarding an exploding table. In " ... Jung's later life, the supernatural was never far away."[7]

The Jungians maintained a mysterious air about the discoveries and theories produced by their master.

According to Hoeller, it amounted to "Hermetic con-
cealment." Carl Jung repeatedly claimed that his theories were based on the empirical evidence from his
own practice of psychiatry. But since Jung was known
to be a gnostic who constantly experienced occult
events, saw ghosts and consorted with astrologers, it
is probable that at least some of the "empirical data"
was discovered by other than purely scientific methods.

Did Dr. Carl Jung promote a doctrine provided to
him by demons? Were his "empirical experiences"
really occultic experiences? It seems so.

It is known that at least one major work of Jung
came directly from an occult experience. Between
1912 and 1917 he went through an "... intense period
of experience which involved a tremendous flooding
of his consciousness from within by *forces which he
called archetypal but which previous ages would have declared to be divine and demonic* [emphasis added]."[8]

During this period Jung withdrew from the world,
except for a small part of his psychiatric practice and
underwent a series of strange inner experiences. He
did not read any books, although previously an avid
reader. He wrote down his " ... strange inner experiences" in some 1,330 pages of handwritten text.

According to the Hoeller account of this period of
Jung's life, his "handwriting at this time changed to
one that was used in the 14th century."[9] He painted
during this period using "... pigments which he himself made, after the fashion of the artists of bygone
ages." Among his most precious possessions was a
red leatherbound volume of these paintings and writings which is now called *Jung's Red Book*.

Neither Jung nor his successors allowed the contents of the *Red Book* to be published, except for a
small excerpt called in Latin *Septem Sermones ad Mor-

tuos (Seven Sermons to the Dead); the work was subtitled "Seven Exhortations to the Dead, written by Basilides in Alexandria, the city where East and West meet." (Note: Basilides was a gnostic writer in hellenic Egypt during the second century A.D.). Although apologists for Jung claim that the book was a "youthful indiscretion" written and signed in the spirit of pseudoepigrapha (a popular practice in ancient times in which a writer assumed the identity of another more ancient writer — which raises hob with scholars), it is likely that he believed that Basilides was, indeed, the author. Again, according to Hoeller: "To Basilides, in fact, does Jung attribute the authorship of the document itself, thus suggesting to some *an element of mediumship and (or) automatic writing* (emphasis added)."[10]

Seven Sermons to the Dead was never intended for the public but instead was published in a private edition for Jung's friends and associates in an attractive, high-quality, red-leather binding. In later years, "Jung himself went on record regarding the contents of the *Red Book* and the *Sermons,* stating that *all his works, all his creative activity has come from these initial visions and dreams and that everything he accomplished in later life was already contained in them*"[Emphasis added].[11]

Continuing with Stephen Hoeller's account: "As one might expect, Jung maintained a constant contact with the mysterious sources that inspired his *Red Book* throughout his life. He remained an inspired — some might say haunted — revelator for the rest of his days."[12]

The writing of *Seven Sermons to the Dead* was mysterious. According to some accounts, it was written in three harrowing nights sometime between December 15, 1916, and February 16, 1917. This book appears to have been written through automatic writing during a period when the Jung family was undergoing a large number of occultic events in their home. Jung constantly felt an ominous presence about him and the Jung children reportedly saw "ghostly entities in the house." Stephen Hoeller's account is perhaps the most graphic in print:

> One of the children dreamt a religiously colored and somewhat menacing dream involving both an angel and a devil. Then — it was a Sunday afternoon — the front doorbell rang violently. The bell could actually be seen to move frantically but no one visable was responsible for the act. A crowd of "spirits" seemed to fill the room, indeed the house and no one could even breathe normally in the spook-infested hallway. Dr. Jung cried out in a shaky and troubled voice: "For God's sake, what in the world is this?" The reply came in a chorus of ghostly voices: "We have come back from Jerusalem where we found not what we sought."[13]

It was then that the *Seven Sermons to the Dead* were born.

Christians being treated by a Jungian psychologist or otherwise involved in Jungian systems (such as inner healing) might well consider the world view and experiences of their originator: the true originator might be something other than a human scientist. Perhaps a biblically based counselor would be more appropriate for most patients.

Jung's belief in experientially relieving psychological problems, characterised by "not out, through the problem," bears more than a superficial resemblance to the gnostic idea of a "Path of Initiation," as told in the Holy Grail epics. In these and other Initiations, the Questor is given a series of tasks or problems to solve (sometimes intellectually) that are designed to bring them to points of crisis or tension. After each segment is successfully negotiated, the Questor is Ini-

tiated to a higher degree — and more tasks or problems. Besides psychology, these methods are common
in gnosticism, mysticism, Zen Buddhism and other
occultic systems.

The evidence of occultic involvement regarding
Jung's mentor, Sigmund Freud, is less convincing.
Nevertheless, it can be demonstrated that Freud was
at least toying with the occultism that he publicly
loathed. Despite statements calling occultism
"creeping black mud," Freud nevertheless consorted
with luminaries of the Occult Revival. In fact, being a
Viennese intellectual in the late 19th- and early 20th-
century period, he could have hardly done otherwise.
Freud regularly visited soothsayers and was friends
with prominent occultists like Wilhelm Fleiss.

According to James Webb: "Freud saw very clearly
the similarities between the occult approach and that
of psychoanalysis."[14]

It is interesting to note that Freud (who was Jewish) was associated with leading occultists of the period, including Georg Lanz von Liebenfels, the Viennese magician whose anti-semitic spasms influenced
the teenaged Adolf Hitler (1908-1913). During the period (1895) when Freud formulated his interpretation
of dreams method, he lived in a house provided by
the Viennese Theosophist Summer Colony.

When psychology began to gain public acceptance,
the Freudians attempted to remove the occultic
strains that were otherwise so evident. It became un-
popular to recall that Freud began working from an
investigation of Mesmerism (hypnotism) and that
Freud associated with occultists. They (including
Freud himself) tried to put the new science on a firm-
er materialistic footing by refering instead to
"psychical research" (parapsychology) in place of
"occultic research." Yet, in later years Freud was ac-

tive in the fields of mental telepathy and edited works in that field of study.

It has been argued that Freud was responsible for secularizing the essentially religious ideas found in the *Kaballa,* the book of Jewish mysticism. While there are similarities, " ... final proof is lacking." It does seem, however, that Freud was indeed involved in beliefs that his followers would consider disreputable and maybe " ... his collection of Egyptian idols ... signify more than antiquarianism ... ".

Conclusion

Psychology has crept into the church and now predominates in many denominations. Major conservative evangelical seminaries have replaced biblical counseling with psychology. Many congregations will not call a pastor to their pulpit unless he had a masters degree (or at least some advanced training) in clinical psychology. Given the demonic origins of clinical psychology and the potential for misdiagnosing organic diseases that are better treated by a psychiatrist (who is a licensed medical doctor), one has to wonder whether psychology has any merit at all. Is it a modern heresy to wonder out loud whether "Christian" psychology is a contradiction in terms — given the rooting of psychology in the New Age?

Drugs, Consciousness and the New Age

It was a Saturday-evening party for college-aged kids and young professionals living in the Virginia suburbs of Washington, D.C.[1] Most of the people brought beer, wine or booze for the "wetting down" at the rowhouse in Alexandria. Because it was the winter of 1966 and marijuana was really illegal in those days, "pot" was there but not evident.

In Virginia at that time, kids drew 20 years in the state penitentiary for possession of mere micrograms of the substance (trace quantities).

The pot smokers, being unsure of the rest of us "straights," would sneak off to a basement workshop to light up in secret. It didn't take a genius to figure out what they were doing, however, because the odor of burning marijuana permeated the house and people returning from the basement had that insipid, vacant look of the thoroughly stoned.

About 10 p.m., the first-floor bedroom where coats were deposited erupted into pandemonium. The screaming and thrashing, crash of splintered furniture and hysterical crying at first sounded like a fight between some of the larger guests. Fifteen or 20 guests crowded into the hallway and bedroom to see four big men trying to restrain a kid who, but for the screaming and crying, looked like he was having a *grand mal* epileptic siezure. The kid seemed to have a superhuman strength as he thrashed about on the bed under the muscles of four would-be NFL linemen.

Later, after the young man was taken to the hospital by his friends, we found out that he had taken LSD and was apparently in the midst of a "bad trip." During his attack, he repeatedly screamed "I've seen the devil! I've seen the devil!" Although I didn't believe him then (I fancied myself an atheist follower of Ayn Rand in those days), I believe him now. It is likely that he saw something he identified as the devil and it frightened him badly. So much so, that a year later he was still under a psychiatrist's care.

That young man was probably not a New Ager (just a dumb kid) but his experience illustrates that drugs can generate spiritual experiences. And not all such experiences are the positive technicolor events reported in the underground "hippie" grapevine of that era.

One aspect of New Age teaching is that certain spiritual disciplines (sometimes called "spiritual techniques" or "psychospiritual technologies")[2] can aid man in discovering his divine self. The New Age view is that man contains a spark of divinity (man is a god) that is smothered inside a physical body. Man can reunite with God only through attainment of knowledge *(gnosis)* of God and his own divine nature. Unfortunately, at our present level of consciousness this is impossible, say the teachings.

An analogy to the level of consciousness problem is a television receiver in a fringe zone a long way from the TV broadcasting station. The receiver is man's consciousness, the antenna is the consciousness-raising disciplines and the TV station is God. In deep fringe zones, the TV picture is all snow and the sound is only a roaring hiss; turn your own TV to a dead channel and crank up the volume to see what it's like. Both sound and snowy picture are noise signals; only occasionally does the signal from God's transmitter break through to paint a washed out black and white picture on the screen of man's consciousness. Fleeting pictures and garbled sound are what man gets from the god-source.

But if we engage in certain spiritual technologies or disciplines to alter our consciousness to a supposedly higher level, it is like placing a huge, electronically amplified TV antenna at the top of a tall tower. The sound and color picture comes through noise free; we have our *gnosis*.

There are several disciplines open to the questor after *gnosis* and all of them are potentially very dangerous. Among the disciplines are: drugs, yoga, visualization, hypnosis, meditation and other methods of mysticism.[1]

Using psychoactive drugs to raise consciousness is as old as man himself.[3] Ever since early man ate the wrong fruit, he has been having such experiences. Drugs are also recognized as among the most dangerous methods, the most crude methods but are also among the most popular methods.

Leading New Age teachers lament drug use and caution their followers not to use this method. The Holy Grail legends, such as *Parsival* by Wolfram von Eschenbach, are among the earliest statements in the proto-New Age Western Esoteric Tradition.[4] Eschenbach learned the Ancient Wisdom from one Kyot of Provence, who cautioned him to "first learn the ABC's ... without the use of black magic." This statement is often taken as a warning against suicidal spiritual shortcuts such as drug use. Yet some New Agers persist in disregarding their own teachers and try drugs.

The drugs used are selected to " ... dislocate man's sense of ordinary reality." By altering consciousness the drugs produce hallucinations, dreams and visions. It seems that we surrender the control of our brain to ghost operators when we ingest those chemical substances. Revelations in the altered state of consciousness are somehow perceived as more real, more valid than ordinary experiences. Thus, the subject of such experiences can be manipulated into thinking he has experienced a spiritual event.

Drug use was very much a part of the Occult Revival of the late 19th century.[5] Marijuana and other substances were in common use and because laws were more lax in those days, there was none of the legal fear that characterized modern drug usage.

Besides marijuana, the anesthetic agents chloroform, ether and nitrous oxide were popular among *avant-garde* Bohemian intelligentsia of the Occult Revival. The use of those agents was so widespread that the movement was dubbed the "Anesthetic Revelation."[6] Anesthesia experimentation was probably more widespread in America than Europe, however.

The leading American proponent was Benjamin P. Blood (1820-1906), whose 1874 book *The Anesthetic Revelation* attracted much positive comment. Blood claimed that the experience was an "initiation ... into the oldest and most intimate and ultimate truth." He also proclaimed that the anesthetic revelation " ... graduated [one] beyond instruction in spiritual things."

Peyote was also in widespread use during the Occult Revival. This drug, which is also called "mescaline" and *"Anhalonium Lewinii,"* is derived from the buds of a cactus flower that are found in the deserts of northern Mexico and southwestern United States. Numerous luminaries of the Occult Revival and the more recent drug subculture, are linked with the use of peyote.

The drug was once distributed freely but today in the United States it is illegal for all but certain American Indian tribes (who use it in religious rituals).[7]

Aleister Crowley, a perverted soul who used many drugs indiscriminantly, also used peyote. According to James Webb, Crowley may have introduced Aldous Huxley to Peyote in pre-1933 Berlin.[8] Twenty years later, Huxley used the same drug under the supervision of a physician and recorded his experiences in his now classic work *The Doors of Perception*.

The European Bohemian subculture was imported into the United States and along with it came the occultism and drugs. There seems to be three main successive periods of American Bohemianism, each one a little less like the European: Original, Beat and Hippie.

The Original period occurred from the 1890s until World War II and involved primarily creative people of the worlds of arts and letters. The Bohemia of that era imported its identity from Paris and the rest of Europe and mixed it with certain native American elements. The center of Bohemia in America of that era was the North Beach area of San Francisco.

Like its European parent, American Bohemianism expressed itself in surrealistic art, American counterparts to German Dadaism and other forms of irrational art. Playwrites, novelists and artists gorged themselves on mystics like Gurdieff, Blavatsky, Hermann Hesse and Eliaphas Levi.

Americanization of imported Bohemian culture transformed the movement into the Beatniks of the 1940s and 1950s. It also broadened the base of the anti-establishment subculture both geographically and demographically. The Beatniks started coming out of North Beach and moved east to New York, settling in Greenwich Village and the Lower East Side. Others settled in the then-not-so-famous Haight-Ashbury area of San Francisco.

There was a different quality to Beatnik culture compared with earlier Bohemians. There was, for example, a wider use of drugs among the Beats. Instead of a peripheral group of drug users, the Beatnik subculture placed marijuana in a central position. There was also a wider tolerance of "tourists" in the movement. These were hangers on " ... who might conform to the expected patterns of behavior, make all the right noises but fail to understand the language.[9]

Perhaps the leading spokesman for the Beat underground in the early 1950s was author Jack Kerouac. His novel *On the Road* created the U.S. version of the myth of the hobo philosopher or "Dharmic bum," who hitchhiked and rode the rails all over the country searching for wisdom.

In Kerouac's hobo we see echoes of the German *Wandervogel* ("wandering birds") of a generation or two earlier. In Kerouac we find hints of adopted Zen Buddhism in the West.

Growing up in the 1950s, I can recall a brilliant science student from my high school who went off to college as a level headed sort of guy to pursue a career in physics. Within 18 months I saw him carrying a book titled *Zen for the Western Man* and mouthing doctrine that shocked his devout Roman Catholic parents. A year later, the young man dropped out of college and spent several years under the care of a psychiatrist.

The Beat subculture added a new dimension to the irrational underground. As a synergism of Bohemian

(Western) occultism, Eastern Hindu and the Zen Buddhist teaching and the traditional protest mindset of its anti-establishment European forefathers, the Beats set themselves up for a transformation of their own. When these elements were blended together with large numbers of drug-oriented hangers-on, a new subculture called "Hippie" emerged. Among the foremost catalysts of the Beat-Hippie transformation was a new substance: Lysergic Acid Diethylamide or "LSD."

LSD was discovered to be a hallucinagenic substance in the spring of 1943 when Doctor Albert Hofmann accidentally absorbed a small amount of the substance. Doctor Hofmann was working on LSD, which is synthesized from fungus ergot, in his laboratory at Sandoz Corporation in Basel, Switzerland. LSD was not illegal in California until June 6, 1966 (6/6/66). Sandoz-made LSD was manufactured in Switzerland, sold to transhippers in Czechoslovakia and then brought into the United States by way of Mexico.

The hallucinations produced by LSD naturally attracted the spiritually oriented among the California anti-establishment subculture. The Beatnik culture was already well advanced in its transformation into Hippie culture and LSD was one of the main catalysts. Although some legitimate scientific experimentation was carried out by medical researchers, most of the imported LSD wound up in the occult-minded Hippie subculture.

Perhaps the grand guru of the LSD crowd was Doctor Timothy Leary formerly of Harvard University. Leary reportedly experimented with mushrooms and a substance called psylocibin until his discovery of LSD around 1961 or 1962. Leary is quoted in Webb's *The Occult Establishment* regarding his LSD experiences: "... I know it is a reality! I know it is the Divine message." According to Webb, Leary then " ... took to frequenting a Hindu *ashram* in Boston." [10]

Although most New Age teachers eschew drug use, there are some who are apparently on a first name basis with Timothy Leary. In early August, 1984, I talked with Constance Cumbey on the telephone. She had just returned from a party at the California home of Marilyn Ferguson (*The Aquarian Conspiracy*). The party seemed to Cumbey like an attempt to win her over to the very cause that she warns of in her book and lectures. She told me that many of the top luminaries of the New Age were present and "... I was close enough to Timothy Leary to snatch the wine bottle out of his hands." The New Age/Drug Culture connection seems obvious.

It's funny how things work out. The reason for my telephone call to Constance Cumbey was to tell her that I had just had an impromptu dinner with New Age spiritual teacher David Spangler. During a trip to A.R.E. (Virginia Beach, Virginia) to research this book, I attended a Spangler seminar.

On Saturday evening, I went to the cafeteria at the Marshalls Hotel for dinner (across the street from A.R.E.).

After sitting down with a group of people, I found that one of them was Julie Spangler's mother, who was babysitting David's and Julie's baby son. David soon walked over and sat down next to me. After a few minutes the other guests left the table and David and I had a 30-minute chat (mostly about Constance Cumbey). When we compared notes later, Constance remarked "What's this? The New Agers take a Fundamentalist to dinner week? ... while you were with Spangler I was at Marilyn Ferguson's house!"

The manufacture of LSD is apparently a somewhat trivial exercise for a knowledgeable chemist. When I was a freshman at Old Dominion University in Virginia, library officials tightly controlled certain chemistry "cookbooks" in hopes of preventing knowledgeable (but not-so-wise) undergraduates from cooking the stuff up in their dorm rooms. One of the primary suppliers to the Haight-Ashbury Hippie community was a mysterious chap called "Owsley."[11]

That the LSD experience, called "psychedelic initiation" by some, was mystical in nature was confirmed by "heroes from the worlds of pop, protest and church [who] testified to the occult significance of the New Age ... ." "In November [1967] the folksinger Buffy Sainte-Marie — who has a degree in the history of religions — proclaimed in Jungian terms: 'I'm dedicated to Satan and Jehovah — my God is [the rooster-headed gnostic god] Abraxas, the god of evil and good.' "[12]

The renegade Episcopal Bishop James Pike testified in September, 1967, that psychedelic experience and mystical Initiation were the same. Bishop Pike converted from a liberal, quasi-orthodoxy to old fashioned spiritism after the death of his son. He once reportedly said he entered a (liberal) seminary as a believer but his theology was taken from him by the seminary and replaced with a "... mere handful of pebbles."

Bishop Pike's life ended when he got lost in the Judaean desert during an expedition, long after he got lost on a spiritual desert of another sort. His tragic experience should be taken as a warning to liberal churchmen that something is wrong with their theology — but it won't.

Illuminated Politics Modern Style

Bohemia in all its forms represents anti-establishment protest. Some protest has been directed against materialist society. Much of the occultist underground that spawned Bohemia was a reaction against the cold rationalism of the Age of Enlightenment and the rise of science. Their protest took the form of a rejection of the established norms of society and took on political overtones that are consistent with anti-materialism.

The later Beatnik culture carried forward the tradition of protest and politics. In the 1930s, Beatnik politics tended toward socialist and communist movements.[13] Throughout the history of Bohemia, protest politics have remained a constant presence. From the social criticism of the Paris underground, to the literature of the Beatnik, to the mind blowing antics of the zany Hippie underground, Bohemia has espoused whatever their society was against (presumedly, Russian beatniks would hold a Capitalist world view).

The basic underlying assumption is that "the Establishment" is always evil and the values of what the Beats called "square society" are corrupt. In this light it is odd that so many Beats were socialists. After all, the USSR is the squarest of square societies and the most hypocritical.

Many people who stay in "straight" society are privately drawn into the anti-establishment subculture on a part-time basis. I can recall Saturday nights in Washington where it was common practice to go up to Dupont Circle and watch the tourists from Pennsylvania ogle the tourists from the Washington suburbs. Hordes of "straight" young people from all over were drawn like insects to the lights of Dupont Circle. Most of them wore wigs to cover their short haircuts so they could return to straight society on Monday morning.

Most of those people were probably materialistic humanists and failed to understand the nature of the Hippie movement. Many never caught the whiff of gas from the Occult Underground of the New Left, which they so admired in secret. The vicarious "straight Hippies" or "tourists" in the Movement threw themselves firmly behind the occultists in the anti-war movement of the later 1960s.

During the 1960s, activists like Jerry Rubin and Abbie Hoffman rallied thousands to the anti-war cause. According to Webb in *The Occult Establishment*: "Rubin moved from the West Coast to New York to become project director of the National Mobilization demonstration at the Pentagon in October, 1967. At that demonstration — for which the *East Village Other* newspaper called for the presence of 'Mystics, saints, Artists, Holymen, Astrologers, witches, sorcerors, warlocks, Druids, hippies, priests, ministers, rabbis, troubadours, prophets, minstrels, bards, roadmen' — a pop group and assorted 'shaman' ostensibly tried to levitate the Pentagon through a semimagical ceremony."[14]

Again from Webb: "During 1969 Abbie Hoffman announced that killing a policeman was a sacramental act. Timothy Leary was interviewed as an expert on sacraments and he voiced his doubts while admitting that it might be 'some people's karma'."[14]

Yoga: Relaxation or Religious Exercise

Many of the former drug users in the New Age Movement graduated to a form of Hindu meditation called "Yoga." Indeed, the transformation from drugs to Yoga is an extremely common occurance. There are also many people who never experimented with drugs but went straight into Yoga. It is also common to find people who are either Christians or have no religion (they are often humanists), practicing Yoga while disclaiming any religious connection. But can we honestly say that Yoga is merely exercise?[16]

Spiritually oriented New Agers report that they experience the same altered state of consciousness as when they used drugs. Like drugs, Yoga is a psycho-spiritual technique used to loosen the person's control over his brain in order to contact or generate as some claim, a Higher Consciousness. The purpose is to discover the divine within oneself. Yoga is occultic and the occultic/spiritual element cannot be disassociated from the exercises.

Hindu *yogis* in the West look with dismay and deep concern at the Westerners who practice Hatha Yoga (one of the more advanced forms) without first going through the preliminary training, which takes years. Yogic exercises are dangerous! Among Hindus, a student is not permitted to practice Hatha Yoga until he has mastered the mental, moral and physical prerequisites. To do otherwise is to invite illness, both physical and mental.[17] The very essence of Yoga is meditation to achieve a detached state. This altered state of consciousness is what permits Sir John Eccles' "ghost" to operate the brain of the *yogi*.

The point of *yogic* exercises is the arousal of *Kundalini*, said to be a serpent representing a female diety, that resides at the base of the spine. *Yogis* claim that there are seven psychic energy centers called *"chakras"* in the spine. These supposed energy centers are dormant or underdeveloped in normal people but can be awakened by the flowing upwards of the supposed *Kundalini* life force. When the *chakra* is awakened, spiritual power is gained. The Hatha Yoga exercises arouse *Kundalini* from her sleep at the base of the spine, to begin the journey of several years duration up the spine through the seven *chakras*.

All practicing *yogis* recognize that releasing *Kundalini* is extremely dangerous. Pain, illness and insanity sometimes await those who practice this form of Yoga. At least one Hindu *yogi* is convinced that most schizophrenics and manic depressives are victims of *Kundalini;* another *yogi* reports that death has occurred when the unprepared attempted Yoga. As innocent an act as prematurely exhausting breath is said to be potentially fatal. *Hatha yoga* is not merely a relaxation exercise!

Hypnotism

Hypnosis is an altered state of consciousness that superficially resembles sleep but is actually nearer the states achieved by meditators and trance mediums. Edgar Cayce, called "the sleeping prophet" by supporters, first learned of his supposed psychic abilities during a hypnotism incident. He was hypnotized by someone who was trying to cure him of a speech problem.

The english words "hypnotism" and "hypnosis" are derived from the Greek *hypnos* (sleep). These words were suggested by 19th-century researcher Doctor James Braid to replace the totally incorrect "animal magnetism" and "Mesmerism" (which reflects the name of the founder of the movement). Although the word "hypnosis" implies sleep, the state is actually quite different from ordinary sleep.

According to Simeon Edmunds:[18]

> Apart from the obvious fact that a sleeping person does not respond when addressed whereas a hypnotized subject reacts to the suggestions of the hypnotist, this difference has been demonstrated by a number of scientific tests and observations.
>
> Reflexes for instance, are usually unchanged by hypnosis (except when suggestions are given that they will change) but are lessened considerably during sleep. The electrical resistance of the body is also unaffected by hypnosis, though it increases by up to ten times during sleep. Recent experiments measuring 'brain waves' by means of electroencephalograph demonstrate the difference conclusively.

There is a wide variation in hypnotic states. Observed differences range from a mild detachment (as if the subject were thinking of something) to a deep mediumistic trance. The victim might be alert or unconscious. The hynotic state brings on a heightened sense of suggestibility, which leads to both amusing and some not-so-amusing happenings. As a response to problems suffered by the victims of stage hypnotists, many jurisdictions either ban or strictly control the circumstances of such performances. Medical and psychological uses are also regulated.

Most people are hypnotizable, although the degree of susceptibility varies considerably. One estimate of the susceptibility of people claims only five to 10 percent of people are "... virtually unhypnotizable." About one-fourth easily go into a deep trance and another group of similar size goes into a light trance. The remaining 40 to 45 percent respond with varying degrees of difficulty. Apparently, hypnosis is a trainable event for some subjects will only achieve a light trance in the first session but go into ever deeper trances in latter sessions.[19]

There is also a wide variability of reactions among hypnotized subjects but it is reasonable to identify three general categories (which I will call Levels) of sensation and reaction: Levels I, II and III representing light, medium and deep hypnosis.[20]

Level I. This state represents light hypnosis and all but five to 10 percent of the population can achieve this level. As mentioned above, 25 percent of the population will achieve this state without difficulty on the first attempt. In *Level I* hypnosis, the subject is drowsy and in deep relaxation. The subject generally feels that he is still in control and could resist the hypnotist's suggestions at any time but rarely does so.

The eyelids and limbs feel heavy and the subject will accept suggestions that he cannot do certain simple things such as moving a limb, opening the eyes or stand up.

Level II. This level is a bit deeper than *Level I*, so results in the subject becoming even more drowsy. Under *Level II* hypnosis, the subject is even more willing to accept suggestions. For example, the subject can be made to hold body positions that would otherwise be uncomfortable or impossible.

A radio talk show host claimed that he was once hypnotized during a stage show and then made to lay rigid with his body supported only at the ankles and shoulders by two chairs. Such a cantilever position is normally impossible to hold for more than a few seconds but the subject in that case held it for more than 15 minutes. The *Level II* subject will accept the suggestion to turn off physical senses such as smell, touch and pain. He will also accept the suggestion of amnesia and will not thereafter remember what transpired while under hypnosis.

Level II is an intermediate level of hypnosis and is the shallowest level under which the subject will accept and act on a post-hypnotic suggestion. Such a suggestion might entail an act to be carried out after the subject is awakened, often upon perceiving a trigger event or word. The post-hypnotic suggestion is sometimes used in supposed therapy for weight control, smoking and so forth.

Level III. The deepest hypnosis is called somnambulism and can result in the subject accepting very complex and often bizarre suggestions. *Level III* is the hypnotic trance state used by stage hypnotists and New Agers doing "past lives regressions" (see Reincarnation Chapter). Under *Level III* hypnosis, the subject may experience vivid hallucinations that involve both the mind and the senses. It is also the state in which alleged psyhic phenomena occur; such as telepathy, clairvoyance and so forth.[21]

The process of hypnotizing someone is called "induction." Although it is probably true that everyone can hypnotize someone, skills vary widely among hypnotists. Contrary to widespread belief, the subject's "will power" has little to do with susceptibility to hypnosis. According to Edmunds, cited earlier, it is generally easier to hypnotize alert, intelligent people than dullards. The easiest to hypnotize are the very people one would expect to be most resistant and have the greatest will power.

Induction methods vary from one hypnotist to another but, in general, all methods require the hypnotist to gain the trust of the subject. It helps if both are believers in the process. The hypnotist will use " ... suggestion to heighten normal suggestibility." The hypnotist will attempt to focus the subject's attention on one thing. It is the focusing that leads to the use of props such as swinging pendulums, flashing lights, slowly spinning color pattern disks and the like. Not all hypnotists use such props, however, and not all subjects are susceptible to all props or all methods. An experienced hypnotist will be sensitive to the subject and be flexible enough to vary the induction method if the subject seems adverse to the method being used.

Some hypnotists use no props whatever to induct their subjects. One hypnotist wrote that he "talks patients down." In *Hypnosis and the Christian* by Martin and Diedre Bobgan, we discover that "talking the patient down" involves a series of deceptions on the part of the hypnotist.[22] In the Bobgan book, the use of "double-bind suggestions" is reported. This is a deception in which the hypnotist always tells the subject that his reaction, no matter what it is, is correct for moving deeper into the hypnotic trance. According to the Bobgans:

> *"Even sincere medical hypnosis may be a disguised doorway and subtle enticement into the demonic realm. It may not be as obvious an entree to evil as occult hypnosis and therefore it could be even more dangerous for an unsuspecting Christian who would otherwise avoid the occult."*[23]

Any Christian who has been hypnotized or, who may be contemplating allowing hypnosis, should read the Bobgans' book first.

Flight to Lucifer

Lucifer! The Morning Star of the New Age! The would-be god represented by the planet Venus (from whence, say the New Agers, he came some 18 million years ago)![1] One of the most chilling aspects to the New Age Movement is its headlong rush to Lucifer. It is not a hidden aspect of the movement for the New Agers are quite open and candid about their Luciferianism.[2]

The Lucifer of the New Age, however, is not the Lucifer of the Bible for the New Agers have divorced Lucifer from Satan and made him something that he isn't. A sanitized Lucifer is presented to the followers of New Age teachers.

C.S. Lewis made an often-quoted observation on two equal errors regarding the devil: one error to is disbelieve in his existence, while the other error is to believe but have too much interest in him.[3] Lewis tells us that the devil doesn't much care which error we make about him so long as we don't see him in his true light.

Even a cursory examination of the New Age Movement causes us to add a third error to Lewis' original two: namely, the error of mis-identifying the devil. That is, making him seem like something that he is not. That third error is the greatest single mistake of the Age of Aquarius because it masks the evil nature of Lucifer.

Understanding the New Age concept of Lucifer requires first an understanding of the New Age cosmology. The study of cosmology is the study of a) the universe as an orderly system and b) the structure and relationships within the universe.

When dealing with New Age cosmology, we need to remember that they mean something more than astronomical or physical universe. The New Age universe is at least partially consistent with the Christian view in that they recognize a spiritual dimension in addition to the physical. It is on the nature of the spiritual dimension that Christians and New Agers disagree.

The New Age Movement generally accepts the theosophical world view. The physical universe is essentially an illusion and it is on the lowest and most dense of seven different interpenetrating realities.[4] The function of everything in the universe is evolution toward higher, less dense, states of being (sometimes identified as "states of consciousness").

The New Age universe seems pointless when it it viewed as an endless procession of cycles. Earths dissolve into new earths, races of beings dissolve into new races (and how much terror that doctrine has caused!) and whole solar systems dissolve into new solar systems. The theosophical doctrines of Rounds and "Wheels within Wheels," govern a seemingly endless process.[5] Ultimately, the biggest wheel of all, the universe itself, dissolves into an infinitesimal contraction and the whole process starts anew.

Creation, in the New Age view, was a colossal mistake; a doctrine that they receive from the ancient Cathari and other gnostic cults. God imprudently created the universe but could neither control it nor destroy it after he realized his error; that New Age god seems hopelessly inept — a view popular with the gnostics.

Another view common in the New Age (they are not consistent) holds that the colossal mistake occurred at the moment of Creation when the created beings were separated from their Creator or "Source." It was the very act of Creation that caused the problem. Since that tragic moment billions of eons ago, man has been trying to return to the Source from an indescribable distance away. The route of return takes man through innumerable reincarnations, governed by the inexorable Law of Karma. In both versions of the myth, we see the unbiblical elements of Creation and the Fall being simultaneous events, with the former being the cause of the latter.

God in the New Age universe is the universe itself. He (or "it?") is said to be a universal or cosmic consciousness. Such a concept is both monistic and pantheistic. It is monistic because it allows only one ultimate reality and requires all elements of the universe be one with all other parts. In other words, "all is part of the universal whole without independent parts." The doctrine is pantheistic because it equates God with the laws and forces of nature and of the universe. God is thus reduced to being a mere force, a law of nature or a principle.

In his book *Reflections on the Christ*, David Spangler teaches that man on earth possesses an "energy of movement" that acts as a kind of gravity that draws inward the material needed not just for physical development but spiritual as well. For his analogy, Spangler uses the demands of a baby for food and other needs for his survival. Spangler calls this inward directed force "creative selfishness." [6]

Spangler further lays out his system by proclaiming that the energies called "creative selfishness" are not just free-floating but are instead " ... embodied by some being." The purpose of that being is to collect the energies (much as a resevoir collects water from the environment, I presume) and then channels them to humans who need them for evolutionary development. On page 36 of *Reflections on the Christ,* David Spangler identifies that being as Lucifer, the " ... angel of man's inner evolution."

One of the laws of the universe tells us that, in the absence of an external ordering force, all systems dissolve from a state of greater order to a state of lesser order.[7] The exception to the rule is the system that is subjected to an external ordering force; such a system can move from lesser order to greater order in seeming contradiction to the universe around it.

So now enter Lucifer — the supreme "ordering force." In the universe of a nonpersonal, immanent god-force, each planet must have its own ordering force to assure and promote its evolution back towards the god-head, i.e., towards orderliness.

According to some New Agers, Lucifer came to earth from the planet Venus 18.5 million years ago (some sources claim 17 million years). He was tasked by the Hierarchy with guiding the souls of earth up the evolutionary ladder toward the god-head and godhood.

Thus, Lucifer in the New Age becomes a kind of bridge or link between man and God — a function Christians thought was given to Jesus Christ.

David Spangler, a man who has been called the "shaman of the New Age"[8] (a term that seems to amuse him) and is probably the leading spokesman for New Age doctrine, tells us concerning Lucifer:

> *"Lucifer prepares man in all ways for the experience of Christhood and the Christ prepares man for*

the experience of God. Jesus said, 'As the Christ, I am the way, the truth and the life. No man goes to the Father but through me.' This is true. The avenue out of microcosmic limitation into macrocosmic wholeness, universal consciousness and attunement is through the Christ. **But the light that reveals to us the presence of the Christ, the light that reveals to us the path to the Christ comes from Lucifer** [Emphasis added]." [9]

Lucifer is thus misidentified and given a positive image in the New Age. But what about the negative image? Christians know a different Lucifer who is one with Satan, the Prince of Darkness. New Agers have divorced Satan and Lucifer. Many of them believe that "Satan" is a myth invented by the church in the Middle Ages, which needed a devil to frighten the vulgar populace into obedience.

Most New Agers who think about Lucifer at all would probably agree with Spangler's explanation of Lucifer's connection with evil. Spangler wrote that some powerful consciousnesses " ... became quite enamoured of ... " the forces and used them as a source of power over others. This discovery and misuse of the forces put the system out of balance.

The evil aspect of Lucifer was not so much from the nature of Lucifer but from man's misuse of his energies. Lucifer is said to be merely the channel of neutral energies that are used for evil by man. According to Spangler's interpretation, Lucifer feels "pain and sorrow and anguish" over human misuse of his energies; *poor guy*.

As man descends into the "inner darkness" of depravity, Lucifer descends with him in order to help him learn to use his Luciferian energies in a responsible manner. The job of Lucifer is to turn the misused energies back on man, causing all manner of pain and suffering, until man finally learns the lesson and turns away from what the *Star Wars* trilogy (Oh, yes!

Star Wars was a New Age production!) called "the dark side of the Force."

Satan's place in this Luciferian process is merely a false creation of man, according to the New Age doctrine. Instead of a real being, Satan is a mere "collective thought form" that is used to explain the misuse of Lucifer's energies.

Christ (or "the Christ" as New Agers like to say) is said to be merely the complement of Lucifer. Not opposed to him, mind you, just acting as a balancing force. The proper analogy might be the christ-weight used to balance the lucifer-weight on a spinning earth centrifuge. Without both weights, the centrifuge machine is unbalanced and will fly apart after only a short time of operation.

The purpose of Lucifer is to create the inner light within man (as "light-bearer"), while the purpose of Christ is to release that light into the world. The release of inner light is said to foster inner wisdom and love, while making room for more inner light (hence increasing spiritual growth potential).

What I consider the most dangerous speculation in Spangler's book is found on page 41. There Spangler tells us that "Lucifer, then, is neither good nor bad in his true essence. He is completely neutral. He is an agent of God's love acting through evolution."

The apparent "bottom line" for man is, according to Spangler, a "Luciferic initiation." This initiation is regarded as the doorway that must be passed to come into the presence of God. The incredible claim is that one must first become a Luciferian in order to know God! What the New Age wants of us is nothing less than Luciferic initiation — which Christians know would deny us salvation.

Thus far, we have been discussing David Spangler's interpretation of the New Age Lucifer. This is a reasonable approach, given his lecture and writing career over the past few years. He is, after all, one of the principal teachers of the New Age Movement.

Let's go to "first sources." According to Madame Helena P. Blavatsky in *The Thesophical Glossary:*

> "*Lucifer (Lat.). The planet Venus, as the bright Morning Star. Before Milton, Lucifer had never been a name of the Devil. Quite the reverse, since the Christian Savior is made to say of himself in Revelations (xvi 22.) 'I am ... the bright morning star' or Lucifer. One of the early Popes of Rome bore that name; and there was even a Christian sect in the fourth century which was called the* Luciferians.*"

The statement above is really a repeat of her charge that Satan received a "bum rap" from the church. In her monumental book *The Secret Doctrine*, which is regarded by many as a New Age scripture, she writes:[11]

> "*Since the church, in her struggle with Manicheanism, invented the devil and by placing a theological extinguisher on the radiant star-god, Lucifer, the 'Son of the Morning,' thus created the most gigantic of all her paradoxes — a black and tenebrous light — the myth has stuck its roots too deep in the soil of blind faith to permit, in our age, even those, who do not acquiesce in her dogmas and laugh at her horned and cloven-footed Satan, to come out bravely and confess the antiquity of the oldest of all traditions.*"

In other words, Lucifer.

Further on in Volume II of *The Secret Doctrine* (p. 511), Blavatsky identifies Lucifer as the same being as known in other societies:

> "*Thus, the true and uncompromising Kabalists admit that for all purposes of Science and philosophy, it is enough that the profane know that the great magic agent called the followers of the Marquis de St. Martin — the Martinists — astral light, by the mediaeval Kabalists and Alchemists the Sidereal Virgin and the Mysterium Magnum and by the Easter Occult-*

ists Aether, the reflection of **akasa** — is that which
the church calls **Lucifer** [emphasis in original]."

Alice A. Bailey, writing in *The Destiny of the Nations*, tells us that Lucifer (called "the Lord of the World") is releasing new energies into the world to bring forth the much-needed "principle of sharing."[12]

Freemasonry is a Luciferic cult, as witnessed by their own words. Consider Albert Pike, writing in his authoritative *Morals and Dogma of the Ancient And Accepted Scottish Rite of Freemasonry:*[13]

"Lucifer, the light-bearer! Strange and mysterious name to give to the Spirit of Darkness! Lucifer, Son of the Morning! Is it he who bears the light and with its splendors intolerable blinds feeble, sensual or selfish souls?"

When one is just beginning to think that Pike is about to put Lucifer in his place, Pike follows the preceding with "Doubt it not!" In other words, he is reaffirming the light-bearer.

Earlier in *Morals and Dogma* Pike tells us concerning Lucifer:

"The true name of Satan, the Kabalists say, is that of Yahveh reversed; for Satan is not a black god but the negation of God. The devil is the personification of Atheism or Idolatry.

"For the Initiates, this is not a Person but a Force, created for good but which may serve for evil. It is the instrument of Liberty or Free Will. They represent this Force, which presides over the physical generation, under the mythologic and horned form of the God Pan; thence came the he-goat of the Sabbat, brother of the Ancient Serpent and the Light-bearer or Phosphor, of which the poets have made the False Lucifer of legend."

Could David Spangler have read Pike's *Morals and Dogma?*

That the New Age, and its sub-group components, are Luciferian cannot be disputed.

Toward One World Religion

... The Bottom Line of the New Age

The plans of the New Age Movement are painfully obvious to even the casual observer. One need not dig deeply to discover what they are about: they will (and do) tell us exactly what they propose. The New Age is working toward a new world order. On the political front, the New Order is expressed as globalism and the desire for a world government based on the United Nations. On the spiritual front it is to be a world religion.

The quest for a world religion makes strange bedfellows for humanists and New Agers seem joined together in their efforts. Humanism grew out of the liberalism movement of a century or more ago. Their background causes them to see factors such as nationalism and dogmatic religion as destablizing forces in the world. Such forces, they reason, can only lead to war and bloodshed. The cure promised by humanism is stability through one-world government and one-world religion.

The world government scheme will take the form of a United Nations presiding in authority over national governments. Various sources promote ideas such as a World Food Authority, World Monetary System, World Medical Authority, redistribution of wealth (by which they mean your property!) and a redistribution of productive capacity.

Some have even suggested dismantling factories in the wealthy countries and reassembling them in Third World countries. Of course, the technicians and engineers needed to make the factories operate will go with them.

Humanists pretend to have a benign, or even positive, view of religion. If you take only some of their words, then it seems that their Global Village will have a place for Christianity and all the other Great Religions. The missing element in their version of tolerance is that religions must stay in their place. All power and authority is in the state and religion must "graciously accept the place allotted to it by the secular authorities."[1]

The words quoted above were taken from an article on pages 13 and 14 in the January/February 1983 issue of *The Humanist* magazine. The article by Seth J. Farber was titled "The Crisis of Secular Authority: Modern Ecclesiastical Responses to the State." Farber pulls no punches in identifying the villains of church/state relations: they are "... right-wing American ecclesiasts" and "... fundamentalist Christianity ..." Later in the article, he further narrows his focus and names those ecclesiasts who would place "... the separation of church and state in dire jeopardy" — it is the Moral Majority and others of like mind.

Farber, who was but 20 years of age when his article was published, wants to see our society compartmentalized regarding secular and ecclesiastical elements. But he reveals more than he knows when he disparages fundamentalists, while at the same time calling liberal churchmen (who are, by fundamentalist standards either non-Christian or barely Christian) "responsible American clerics." The implication is that only "safe" churches will be tolerated in Farber's utopia. Presumedly, fundamentalists and other Bible-believing churches will be suppressed for the good of society.

What do you suppose will be the criteria for "safe" churches? Farber doesn't say but other humanists and liberals have spoken out on the matter. They continuously lament Christians who seek to impose their beliefs on others. What they fail to state, for it shows them guilty of the same crime they lay at our door, is that all political processes involve imposing someone's values on someone else.

When the Christian wants to impose an anti-abortion value on humanists he is overstepping the bounds of religion; but when the humanist imposes a pro-abortion value on the Christian it is fine and dandy.

The same issue of *The Humanist* carried an article titled, "A Religion for a New Age," by John J. Dunphy.[2] The author takes a few not so original swipes at Christianity and then drags the reader through several inflammatory paragraphs designed to make the reader believe that the church is a bloodthirsty monster. It is difficult for Dunphy to argue from first principles, so he piles allegation upon allegation in an effort to support his claims. By ample use of "the argument from selected instance," he pretends that the corrupt elements of the church, which any 2,000-year old movement will have many, convinces the reader that his picture truly defines the church. He informs the reader of his opinion of the Bible using words like "outmoded" and "archaic" and then follows that one-two punch with the assertion that it remains "... an incredibly dangerous book." The Bible is supposedly responsible for every bad thing in Western culture for the past two millenia!

The short biography of Dunphy given at the end of the article tells us that he is interested in the study of Christian gnostics and the Ancient Mystery/fertility cults. Even without the biography, however, we would be able to discern Dunphy's interest from the position he proclaims in the article. His religion is a humanism "... that recognizes and respects the spark of what theologians call divinity in every human being." This sentiment accurately reflects the New Age "divinity of man" doctrine.

The aspect of Dunphy's article that should chill Christians the most is his recommendation that humanist teachers — from preschool to universities — teach Humanism to our children. He openly — and correctly — identifies the classroom as the battleground.

There is a great deal of crosslinking between the Globalists of the humanist movement and the New Age Movement. The networking principle brings together many diverse interest groups. What may surprise the humanists is that the New Age concept of One World Religion differs markedly from their own — except of course those humanists who are also *bona fide* New Agers.

New Agers believe that mankind is on the brink of massive planetary, spiritual and social changes. One of those changes will be inauguration of a single religion for all of mankind. Some of them talk about the New Religion overthrowing the old in terms that hint of violence. Most New Agers, however, teach that the new will overcome the old by a gentler process of ecumenical unity and absorption of the religions into one another.

Those who teach a unity of the world's religions foresee a "religious United Nations" form of structure in which Hindu, Moslem, Buddhist, Jewish,

Christian and other religions participate equally. The New World Religion will contain all the common elements of all religions, while retaining distinctives.

The basis for this One World Religion is the claim that all the major religions currently in existence teach variations of the same doctrine. It is claimed that the Ancient Wisdom is at the base of all religions. Over the centuries, each religion modified the true doctrine so much that each is but a distorted variant of the true Ancient Wisdom.

In some cases, Christianity, for example, distortion was intentional. They claim that the church fathers deleted references to the Ancient Wisdom from the Bible. The same charge could be made of Rabbinic Judaism because they use the same Scriptures that Christians call the Old Testament.

What will the new religion of the New Age be like? Although certain details differ according to the commentator, the ideas of Benjamin Creme seem widespread enough to serve as a general model. In his book *The Reappearance of the Christ and the Masters of Wisdom*, Creme tells us that the New World Religion will fuṣe East and West to synthesize something new. It will also fuse the seemingly contradictory concepts of God Immanent and God Transcendent.[3]

Creme is crystal clear regarding the basis of the world religion. It will be based on the Ancient Mysteries, which means that the New Age religion will be held together by a common mystical experience. It is this common mystical experience that is the glue that holds the New Age Movement together. The New Age Movement brags about their unity in diversity. There are so many New Age groups of such widely varying focii and interests that the movement is very difficult to pin down. But there is a common factor: mystical experiences.

Creme also reports that Invocation will be a big factor in the New Age religion. The word "Invocation" infers calling on authority, petitioning for help (both of which explain its use in prayer). According to one dictionary, however, invocation is also a formula for conjuring. When the New Agers repeat the Great Invocation they are attempting to conjure up a demon called Lord Maitreya.[4]

In its true essence, therefore, the invocation by a New Ager is little more than summoning a demon! Creme boasts that one day the Great Invocation will be a "world prayer" and that it is already used by millions of people.

The New Age religion will require Intiation, according to Creme and others. Given the nature of the New Age Movement — it is a Luciferic Movement — it takes very little effort to guess that the Initiation will be a Luciferic Initiation.[5]

In the religion of the New Age, the "esoteric process of Initiation" will occupy a central role. Creme claims that Initiation is a scientific process by which he apparently means a merely "knowable" process rather than a hard science, like physics, that is the most sacred ceremony of the new religion. Two of the three Initiations will occur in the physical plane in New Age temples. The third Initiation (demon possession?) is said to take place in a spirit realm.

The purpose of Initiation is to help the individual (and mankind in general) enter the Hierarchy — called by Creme "the kingdom of God" — and get much closer to divinity than is possible in the physical plane.

The celebrations of the New Age religion will be the New Age festivals promoted by the followers of Alice Bailey: Easter Festival (but not the Christian version!), Wesak Festival and Christ Festival (one month after Wesak).[6]

In the Creme scenario, the other world religions will simply wither away slowly as converts turn to the new religion and old practicers of old religions die off. Given end times prophecy, I wonder how Benjamin Creme will explain away the Rapture of the Church?

Another view of the New World Religion is provided to us by Dr. Lola Davis in her book *Toward A World Religion for the New Age*.[7] Davis was once a missionary to India where she and her husband served. Lola Davis' short biographical sketch on the back cover tells the story of a fundamentalist Christian woman who became enamoured of Eastern religions while on the mission field and thereby fell into what orthodox Christians regard as heresy.

Davis repeats the New Age claim that there is an underlying unity in all of the world's religions. In her "Synopsis of Toward a World Religion for the New Age,"[8] she calls the Ancient Wisdom by the alternate name the "Ageless Wisdom" but it is the same old New Age doctrine.

In the Synopsis, Davis tells us that all religions wait for a very special personage: Christians await Jesus Christ, the Jews await Messiah, Moslems await Imam Mahdi and the Eastern religions await Lord Krishna or Bodhisattva.

New Agers teach that all of these are the same person as Lord Maitreya. Christians are tempted to see another sort of world spiritual leader in the New Age scenario: antichrist. Although Christian believers should be able to recognize an antichrist, many believers of other religions may be taken in by Lord Maitreya.

The New Age thrust toward a world religion has

been going on for a long time. Lola Davis tells us that she found that "... much thought and planning" had been done already. Lucis Trust, the organization of Alice Bailey, marketed Davis' book in 1984 when I bought my copy.

David Spangler tells us in *Reflections on the Christ* that entrance into the New Age requires a Luciferic Initiation.[9] Lucifer is said to offer man wholeness and the Luciferic Initiation is acceptance of Lucifer's offer. The problem the New Agers fail to see, however, is that act could lead one irrevocably to eternal hell.

The disposition of the church (and presumedly other religions that don't want to be integrated into the New Age) is not altogether clear in New Age writings. A few people — very few, fortunately — suggest a sudden, violent end for Christianity. Some of the more inflammatory people claim that the new cannot manifest until the old is out of the way. Most teachers are somewhat gentler in their predictions of our fate. The usual teaching is that the church will slowly decay and wither away.

David Spangler presents a teaching that may refer to the church in the New Age.[10] In his book *Revelation: The Birth of a New Age* he describes the fate of those souls who are either not ready or not compatible with the New Age. Spangler likens earth to a mansion with many floors, with the physical plane being the ground floor. Higher floors represent higher, nonphysical, planes. Those who cannot enter the New Age correctly would be transfered to one of those upper floors. If the church is included, then the implication is that the church will disappear to some higher spiritual realm. What an explanation for the Rapture! When millions of Christians disappear, the New Agers can claim that we were zapped to some other dimension so that the New Age can be inaugurated.

In a peculiar kind of way that most of them fail to understand, that's exactly what will happen! I suspect that their "New Age" will last only seven terrifying years and then will be followed by the return of the real Christ, not their false christ Lord Maitreya.

One world religion or one that is at least trans-Western encompassing all of the previously Christian countries, is prophesied in Revelation and other books of the Bible. It comes as no surprise, therefore, that the goal of the Great Delusion is one religion — a non-Christian religion — for all the world.

What Should Christians Do?

The response of the church to the New Age Movement is critical to millions of people because their eternal salvation is at stake. But before deciding what we must do, let's first spell out what we should not do. It is claimed that the New Age Movement heralds the antichrist. Even if this speculation is true, we should not overemphasize this aspect to the detriment of other aspects. If this is truly the time that God has selected to permit the rise of antichrist, then there is nothing at all that we can do about it — nor should we want to. Antichrist will come according to God's timetable, not ours.

My own opinion is that the New Age Movement is part of a centuries-long softening up process and this Great Delusion will ultimately result in a world that is ripe for antichrist.[1] But whether the time is five years or five centuries, I am not prepared to speculate. After all, the New Age Movement has existed in its modern form for 110 years and preaches a doctrine that is several millenia old (which is why they call it the "Ancient Wisdom").

We also must not fear the movement. After all, if you will permit me to paraphrase scripture: He that is in us is greater than he who is in the New Age Movement.

Our plan of action requires four aspects: awareness, evangelization, refutation and an emphasis on sound doctrine among our own people. We need to be aware of the New Age, its doctrines, its activities, its goals and its methods. Part of this aspect is educational activities such as reading the various books on the movement that are now on the market. You should arrange to show films such as *Gods of the New Age*[2] and *Pathway to Paradise*[3] in your church.

Seminaries, Bible colleges and Christian colleges should sponsor workshops and seminars and offer courses on the New Age Movement. No longer is it reasonable for them to cover all of the heresies and cults from the death of John to the present time in a single course. All of these activities raise our general awareness of the movement.

Pastors, teachers, elders and other leaders must be made aware of the movement. I was told about one pastor who read a news item about a church conference on the New Age Movement in *Christianity Today* and then sneered that it was "only the same old paganism." Implicit in his comment is "... so we don't have to do anything about it."

There are at least two errors in calling the New Age Movement "...just the same old paganism." First, it's technically incorrect or at least only partially correct. Second, even if the statement were entirely true, the immense size of the movement today warrants massive Christian action to counter its effects.

That brings us to our second and third responses to the movement: evangelization and refutation.

Evangelization is needed because people in the New Age Movement and people attracted to it are damned for placing their hope for salvation in a false system. Evangelism is the art and practice of spreading the Gospel of Jesus Christ and that is what New Age questors need most of all.

Refutation is merely the art of practical apologetics. We must train ourselves in apologetics so that we can counter the arguments of the New Age. Unfortunately, this is a bigger task than might be imagined. Our biggest fault in this area is a history of loose thinking; we have become intellectually shabby.

Too many people in the church regard doctrine and theology as dry, dusty subjects to be considered only by seminary professors and pastors on the upper levels of the intellectual spectrum. But that is not true, for doctrine is the formal basis for our opinions and beliefs. If we do not maintain good doctrine, then all manner of bad teachings can creep into the church. It is the lack of good doctrine, upheld by elders and pastors of the church, that has caused so many to slip into error. We cannot hope to counteract the New Age when our own sloppy thinking leads us to teach and do exactly the same things in our assemblies.

It is essential that church leaders understand the New Age Movement and be able to offer proper, biblically based apologetics to counteract both the influence of New Age doctrine that infects the body and the teachings that keep non-Christians from salvation. It is important to remember that the very people who are deceived by New Age doctrines are prime candidates for the Christian witness of the Gospel because they are already seeking something spiritual. Thus, the New Age Movement offers an unprecedented evangelism opportunity.

Shirley MacLaine and others have had a tremendous influence.[4] We need to come against that teaching in love and understanding and direct New Age questors (including MacLaine) toward eternal life in Jesus Christ ... not the endless progression of meaninglessness offered by the Luciferian New Age Movement.

And Who Do You Say I Am?

Prologue

Do you know the answers to these questions:

- *What is the most important religous question?*
- *Was Jesus a magician?*
- *What about the missing 18 years?*
- *Was Jesus an Essene?*
- *Did Jesus have an Indian (Hindu) connection?*
- *What or who is "The Christ?" Christ or Krishna?*
- *What do the scriptures say? Why is this question important?*

The New Age Movement has brought into sharp focus the critical question of the identity of the Christ. Even some (mostly liberal) Christian groups today have erroneous ideas concerning the Christ. Eastern religions have made inroads into Western culture and have brought their own identities for the Christ. With most of the world awaiting the coming of a messiah-like figure, it becomes terribly important for us to learn the truth regarding this future figure — for his coming will mark the major turning point of all history.

The Problem

Jesus. That name is never neutral! The name "Jesus" inspires either worship or hostility from virtually everyone. No one, at least in Western countries, is dispassionate towards Jesus. The reason is that no religious question is ultimately more important than the identity of Jesus.

Christianity stands like a lonely tree outside the forest of religions and the main issue that separates it from the rest is the means of salvation. In most other religions, a person *earns* salvation through some kind of *works*. In some religions, it is the performance of certain duties that makes the difference. In others, it is good deeds and philantropy. In Hindu and most New Age religions, good works and suffering are needed to rub off "bad karma" over a long series of reincarnations. But in Christianity, salvation is by *grace* — there is no other way.

Some religions attempt to combine works and grace by claiming that a person earns grace through a long progression of good works and spiritual development (especially the latter). When the person reaches the proper level of achievement, God smiles kindly on the Questor and confers grace as a reward. Supposedly, God's grace erases the remaining bad karma owed by that soul. This viewpoint is nonsense because it contains a contradiction in terms. According to the dictionary, grace is an *unmerited* gift of divine assistance or favor; grace, therefore, can *never* be earned.

It is salvation by grace that makes the identity of Jesus so critically important. Unless Jesus is who he claimed to be, then he is not qualified to offer grace to anyone; his death and resurrection are meaningless. Therefore, if Jesus is not who and what he claimed to be, then Christianity has no basis.

This is the reason why so many people attack Christianity while tolerating other religions. That is also why so many other religions pay peculiar attention to a Jesus whom they would otherwise find so easy to dismiss; and it is also why the single most important question in scripture is " ... and who do you say I am?"

Who Do They Say He Is?

Author Tal Brookes wrote an answer to many of the "life after life" experiences reported in popular (even Christian) literature. One of his comments in *The Other Side of Death* is most revealing. He states that the so-called "beings of light" encountered on the "other side" have an inordinate interest in Jesus.[1] It is a level of interest far out of proportion to his real importance if he is who or what *they* say he is!

So who is he? Let's discuss the claims of both Christians and non-Christians regarding the identity of Jesus Christ. Some of these views are held by liberal Christians, while other views which we will examine are held by non-Christians. The only criterion to apply in deciding which opinion is the best is "which one is most probably correct."

It is amazing how many guises are thrust upon Jesus. To the liberal Christian he was a "Great Moral Teacher." Higher criticism has so eroded the faith of liberal churchmen that they can see him only as a man offering profound teachings — if he existed at all.[2] Let's examine this and other teachings about Jesus.

According to certain Jewish rabbinic lore, Jesus was not virgin-born at all but, rather, was the son of a man named Pantera. In the late first century A.D., a Jewish rabbi named Eliezer promoted the same myth that is with us even today. Eliezer may have been referring to a real person when he called Christ "Jesus ben Pantera."

In Bingerbrueck, Germany, there is a first-century A.D. tombstone of a Sidonian archer named Tiberius

Julius Abdes Pantera. This man was from Sidon, a city that still exists up the coast from Israel in present-day Lebanon. He was a soldier in the Roman Legions and served both in Palestine and the Rhenish provinces of Germany.

The name "Jesus ben Pantera" means "Jesus, son of Pantera." During the Nazi era Pantera's tombstone became the focal point of Goebbels' propaganda effort to dejudaize Jesus. Hitler held Jesus in high esteem and compared himself favorably with Jesus.[3] It was necessary for the Nazis to dejudaize Jesus in order to fit their sick racial doctrines. The Nazis claimed that Mary was either a Moabite or Elamite woman who was raped or seduced by a Rhenish (German) Roman soldier and that Jesus ben Pantera was the resultant offspring. Thus, Jesus was effectively dejudaized in the German mind and even made into a German — which supposedly accounted for his superiorty over other men. It is indeed ironic that the greatest persecutor of the Jewish people in all of history, Adolf Hitler, would have used Rabbi Eliezer's testimony to dejudaize Jesus!

The "Adoptionist" school of thought holds that Jesus was an ordinary man until God adopted him as his son. According to this view, Jesus perfected himself through various spiritual disciplines until he was a suitable habitation for the "Christ Consciousness." At that time, the Holy Spirit descended and took over the body of a mortal Jesus, who then became the immortal Son of God. The adoption supposedly took place at the Jordan River when Jesus was baptized by his cousin John.

There is also a school of thought that claims that Jesus was an Essene, while another claims that he was a magician in competition with the likes of Simon Magus. He is allowed to be anything at all except the divine Son of God. Many New Age people will tell you that Jesus is divine but just as you think that a glimmer of biblical truth is peaking through the fog it becomes painfully apparent that they believe that Jesus is "divine" the same way that *all* humans are "divine."

Modern occultists would tell you that Jesus was an "Initiate" into the Ancient Mystery religions. Still other occultists claim that Jesus was one of the "Masters of Wisdom."[4] An Initiate is a person accepted by those who allegedly control occult knowledge and the "ancient wisdom" and who is supposedly given access to such knowledge when it is denied to others. There are levels or "degrees" of initiation and the Initiates are ranked according to the level of knowledge that is either attained or conferred. Various systems have three, five, seven or nine levels of initiation; modern Freemasonry, itself an occultic initiation religion, has 33 degrees.

The "Masters of Wisdom," also sometimes called "Hidden Masters" or "Ascended Masters," are allegedly transhuman beings who were formerly human but who have evolved beyond the need for physical bodies. The Masters no longer need to reincarnate into the physical plane but, rather, can further their own evolution on higher (nonphysical) planes.

According to occult lore, each planet is ruled by a small group of selected Masters who are assigned to direct that planet's evolution. There are supposedly 63 Masters assigned to guide man's ascent to godhood on earth. The secret, nonphysical places occupied by the Masters correspond to certain remote physical locations on earth, such as Shamballa in the Gobi Desert and Wesak Valley in the Tibetan Himalayas. More recently, the Andes of South America (especially Peru) are claimed as a habitat for the Masters.

The Masters are said to occassionally incarnate for a short trip into the physical plane. They allegedly borrow a physical body for that period — a process that most Christians would recognize as demon possession.

According to some New Age writers, Jesus is one of the Masters and lives in Wesak Valley with certain other former "christs." One New Age source claimed recently that the former christ, Jesus, is now living in Rome to await the imminent appearance of the present "christ," Lord Maitreya.

Most of the revisionist opinion regarding Jesus' identity rests on one of two false premises. First, that scripture is not divinely inspired, not inerrant and not to be trusted either literally or as historically accurate. Second, that the power-hungry early church authorities made an intentional effort to conceal errors in their doctrine by forcibly suppressing "scripture" documents that told the truth but did not agree with the official papal "party line."

The first view is prefered by liberals who need it in order to make their system work. The second is the ploy of theosophists and other New Agers to make room for their favorite doctrines. Unfortunately, the second view is given some credit by the fact that the post-Constantine church routinely destroyed the documents of the gnostics and other heretics. New Agers claim that the destruction of those books by church authorities was done not so much to contain heresy but rather to cover up their own heresies instead.

In the sections to follow we will reveal what the various sects claim for Jesus and then finish our discussion with a statement of what Jesus claimed for himself.

Jesus the Magician

Some critics claim Jesus was a "Magi" or ritual magician and that is exactly how some people see him today! This view probably came out of the same 19th-century "Occult Revival" which spawned robed ritual magicians all over Europe (Crowley, Lanz, etc.) and perhaps also from the Higher Criticism movement that needed to de-deify Jesus in order to justify itself.

When the liberal churchman is confronted with biblical miracles he has to either discount them altogether (as merely folk tales or lies invented by Christians) or present them as the activity of some kind of magus (although not necessarily with the supernatural interpretation of the reported magical phenomena).

The problem is made easier for liberals by the fact that they do not consider scripture inerrant. In fact, most of them seem to regard the Gospels as a mere confession of faith instead of a historical account of what actually occurred. It therefore becomes easy to shoehorn Jesus into the magi mold.

To the ancients, "Magi" did not mean the public performer of mere tricks (a stage magician or illusionist). The Magi was a worker of miracles, a controller of the natural and supernatural forces and the performer of powerful religious rituals. The Magi was also custodian of the "Ancient Wisdom" that was taught in the mystery religious schools.[5] Perhaps the closest equivalent to the Magus in our modern context is the primitive shaman.

Several events are cited as evidence by the proponents of the "Jesus as magician" viewpoint. For example, there is the story of the wise men who visited the infant Jesus. These men were said to be Chaldeans (Magi) from the East (Babylon). The claim is made that the three wise men recognized Jesus as the king of the Magi, a reincarnated "Higher Initiate." It is also claimed that the miracles performed by Jesus were mere parallels of "miracles" performed by other known Magi: healing, resurrections (the Lazarus event), control over nature and authority over demons.

They also note that baptism was a rite used by mystery cults of that era and that those cults tended to stress ritual magic. One of the proponents of the Magi view is Dr. Morton Smith, who wrote a book titled *Jesus the Magician*.[6] Dr. Smith also wrote *The Secret Gospel*,[7] a book that claims to reveal previously unknown but valid portions of the Gospel of Mark.

The Missing 18 Years

Scripture is silent regarding the 18 years when Jesus was a youth. We see him in the Gospels as a 12-year-old confounding the elders in the Jerusalem temple with his knowledge and wisdom.[8]

Our next picture is Jesus near the age of 30 years about to begin his public ministry. Those missing 18 years are used by critics to explain their own answers to the question of Jesus' identity.

There is an unasked question in all of the explanations for the missing 18 years: Why do we need an extraordinary explanation in the first place? All of the explanations offered for those missing years depend on either undocumented speculations, poorly documented legends or bizarre interpretations of legends that have less extraordinary (hence more reasonable) explanations. If Jesus is truly who he claimed to be, then no 18-year "initiation" would be needed — a viewpoint that supports the Christian contention that Jesus spent an uneventful 18 years as a carpenter in Galilee.

Surprisingly, both liberals and neo-gnostics are fond of making Jesus into a member or "fellow traveler" of the various mystery religions. Some people accept the Essene theory, while others like to send Jesus on journeys to either Egypt (to study in the Alexandrian mystery schools) or to India (to study Hindu religion). A few commentators send an "Essene" Jesus to both Egypt and India for the missing years. Let's examine the Essene connection.

An Essene Jesus?

The Essenes were a Jewish religious community that existed in Palestine over a period of time that included both the lifetime of Jesus and the founding of the church. The Essenes were desert dwellers who separated themselves from the rest of Israel to practice asceticism and a brand of austere righteousness. They were pacifists who shunned the temple sacrifice of the Pharisees and maintained a gnostic religion that included elements transplanted from Babylon and other Eastern nations.

When a man entered the Essene community he was required to undergo baptism and had to swear to live a life of truth and righteousness.[9] All property in the community was held in common and work was divided according to skills and gifts of the individuals. The Essenes were probably quite scholarly for their libraries were impressive. The Dead Sea Scrolls, found at Qumran near Jerusalem, are apparently from a nearby Essene community.[10]

According to some scholarly opinion, the manuscripts found at Qumran were deposited there for safekeeping when the community was under attack. Dates for the event sometimes cited are 50 A.D., the First Revolt (A.D. 66-71) and the Second Revolt (A.D. 132-135). It was during the First Revolt that the Roman legions of Titus razed Jerusalem and destroyed the Temple.

Some sources give a much later date that coincides

with the struggles between the church and the gnostic heresies. This later date is reasonable for the Nag Hammadi codices discovered in Egypt but is probably erroneous for the Dead Sea Scrolls.

According to both New Agers and certain liberal Christians, Jesus spent a considerable portion of his "lost" 18 years residing in an Essene community, possibly the one at Qumran. Supposed proof of this connection is the fact that some Essene teachings parallel Christian teachings. The Rev. Dr. Charles Francis Potter supports this view in his book *The Lost Years of Jesus Revealed,* a copy of which I purchased in a New Age bookstore.[11] Dr. Potter reveals an unfortunate, sarcastic attitude towards conservative Christians by his sneering comments. He also reveals quite a bit at the end of his book where he calls the Dead Sea Scrolls "God's gift to the humanists."

There are several possible criticisms of Dr. Potter's view. First, Potter and other liberals attempt to "demythologize" Jesus into a mere man, not the Son of God. A conclusion that can be drawn from this view is that no spirit world exists — an implication that even some supporters of that view are loath to admit. If Christian doctrine was lifted from earlier sources, then Jesus can be safely dismissed — which is perhaps the real reason for the adamant essenization of Jesus.

Second, the "Essenic origin of Christian teachings" viewpoint rests precariously on narrowly dating the Dead Sea Scrolls at or immediately prior to the time of Jesus. While many critics would otherwise jump to point out that manuscript dating without hard external archaeological or historical evidence is a much flawed, inexact process at best. They flinch when the same point is made concerning the Dead Sea Scrolls or the gnostic codices from Nag Hammadi in Egypt.[12]

In the absence of a firm date within the text of the manuscript, only guesses can be made regarding its actual age. While such guesses are usually the product of diligent scholarship by honest researchers, they can still be off by centuries, let alone the few decades that are required to date the Dead Sea Scrolls after the rise of first-century Christianity.

One must keep in mind that scholars are not perfect and scholarly opinion changes often — with and without additional proof. The world of the scholars is sometimes testy, as learned men with doctoral degrees square-off to fight over minutia. Laymen sometimes hold scholars in awe and gild their pronouncements with the halo of gospel truth — only to be disappointed when reading of their squabbles.

One must give respect to men of learning, to be sure, but one must also recognize that they are merely men making educated guesses that are based on admittedly incomplete information. Sometimes, the adamant refusal to budge from their previous position is due to a need to maintain their reputation in a "publish or perish" world rather than a concern for the truth.

Even though a permissable date for the Dead Sea Scrolls internment is 50 to 70 A.D., no great damage is done to the conservative Christian position by this dating. The liberal position is devastated by that dating, however. The liberals require a decent interval of time between the death of all eyewitnesses to Jesus' ministry and the writing of the Gospels (which are the record of that ministry). That way, they can boast that the miracles reported in the Gospels are no more than folk accretions to an error-filled oral tradition.

Recently, however, Jesuit priest José O'Callahan — an expert on ancient manuscripts — identified fragments from a cave near Qumran (close to where the Dead Sea Scrolls were found) as coming from the Gospel of Mark.[13] According to both secular and Jewish scholars, the cave was sealed not later than 50 A.D., so now we have a Gospel of Mark manuscript fragment from a time when there were still numerous eyewitnesses alive to refute its claims.

Does early dating of the Dead Sea Scrolls harm the conservative position? Does pre-dating Christian ideas produce any mortal wound to conservative theology (the Mark fragments could raise that question)? No it doesn't for if Christian doctrines are indeed eternal truths, as they claim, then many of them would be contained within the Old Testament. Since such ideas were part of Judaism in the pre-Christian era, then it is likely that a community of scholarly, righteous Jewish "monks" would re-discover them in their scripture, practice them in their lives and mix them with the Eastern accretions that are so evident in their legacy.

The existence of parallels between Essenism and Christianity merely points out that eternal truths are eternal truths, rather than shaking the foundation of the church. Thus, the existence of Essene teachings parallel to Christian teachings tends to prove the truth of those teachings — not that they are somehow borrowed from other traditions.

The most profound flaw in the "Essene Jesus" theory is its total lack of documentation. Proponents claim that Jesus was the Essene "Teacher of Righteousness" or perhaps a composite of several such teachers. This opinion is held despite the fact that other scholars maintain that the Teacher of Righteousness lived 50 to 100 years before Jesus. Besides, if Jesus were the Teacher of Righteousness, why isn't he mentioned by name in Essenic literature? Also, why don't any of the New Testament records call Jesus by that title? His leadership of a major sect like the Essenes would certainly be pertinent to the Gospel writers. Proponents of an Essenic Jesus sometimes maintain that the early church altered the Gospels — a position that we will deal with below.

The Indian (Hindu) Connection

Another view of Jesus that is popular among those who have a need to demythologize Jesus is that he spent those missing 18 years studying Hinduim and Buddhism in India. Edgar Cayce, the supposed Christian who gave "readings" while in a trance, believed that Jesus learned advanced spirituality while on journeys to the East. A popular book on this theme (Janet Bock's *The Jesus Mystery*) has a front cover that depicts a meditative "Jesus" sitting in the *yogic* "lotus" position amid towering mountain peaks that remind one of the Himalayas.[14]

Bock's book reports that a Russian nobleman named Nicolas Notovitch made an extensive tour of Afghanistan, India and Tibet during the late 1880s. Notovitch set down his memoirs in a book titled *The Unknown Life of Jesus Christ (New York, 1890)*.

Notovitch suffered an accident while in the Himalayas and had to recuperate at Himis Buddhist Monastery in Ledak, Tibet. During his convalescense, a Buddhist monk showed him a manuscript written in the ancient Pali language. The story told on the manuscript was about a young man named "Saint Issa" whose life story parallels that of Jesus. The Saint Issa manuscript gives details of Issa's life between the ages of 12 and 30 years, a fact that pleases critics of orthodox Christianity.

No one from the outside world saw the manuscript again after Notovitch until 1922, when an Indian viewed it. Unfortunately, the manuscript disappeared from Western scrutiny and because of the Red Chinese invasion and occupation of Tibet it is unlikely to resurface anytime soon. Our only record of what it said was the translation given in Notovitch's 1890 book.

According to the legend, young Issa left Nazareth at the age of 13 and traveled to India. The journey was financed by his mother, who sold all of her household goods. Issa traveled through what is now called Iraq, Iran (old Persia), along the Persian Gulf and the western shore of the Arabian Sea to Sindh, Pakistan. At Sindh, Issa met with and joined the Jains.[15] Those people practice an austere religion that derived from Hinduism about the same time as Buddhism. Their teachings include vegetarianism, nonviolence, good works and celibacy.

Saint Issa left the Jains at Sindh and traveled to India, where he settled for six years at Jagannath Temple in Puri to study Hinduism. During this time Issa became a perfect *yogi*. That status supposedly gave him the ability to perform the miracles reported in the Gospels. These powers (called *siddhis* by Hindus) are cited by some people to explain away the miracles of Jesus.

While Christians believe that the miracles reported in the Gospels were performed to establish his divine credentials, the New Ager would tell you that they were merely manifestations of *siddhis* by a perfected *yogi* named Issa or Jesus.

Issa supposedly matured spiritually while in India and reached the stage of evolution called "Christ Consciousness" by New Agers. It was this spiritual status that later permitted the Christ to possess the body of Jesus.

When Issa attained Christ Consciousness at the age

of 25 he became an Avatar. But interestingly enough, those who de-christify Jesus only grant him status as a Fourth Degree Initiate. This not-quite-perfected status means that he was very powerful but still had to go through a few more reincarnations (which means that Jesus still needed physical bodies). He is still alive, as the Christians say, but the New Agers mean in the physical world. Some New Agers will tell you that Jesus is still alive on earth after 2,000 years and lives in the Himalayas with the other Masters of Wisdom. Some have recently claimed that Jesus moved to Rome in preparation for the manifestation of Lord Maitreya. He will allegedly take over the Vatican and become a future pope. They claim that Jesus is currently in a 600-year-old Syrian body gained in a reincarnation later than the incarnation written of in Scripture.

Issa left India at the age of about 30 and returned to Palestine by way of Tibet, Iran and southern Russia. It was on his return to Israel from India, say some New Agers, that Jesus began the public ministry that is recorded in the Gospels.

As in the case of the Essene Jesus, there are neither Jewish nor Christian source documents to support the Indian Connection. Although church alteration of the record is a possible explanation, as some would have it, this claim suffers the same fate as other alteration theories.

Christ or Krishna?

Much is made of the similarities between Jesus Christ and the Hindu's Lord Krishna. It is implied that the Jews adopted Krishna to their own use and that Christianity is thus based on Hinduism. Implicit in this view is that Christians debased the truth and buried the true Lord Krishna in Jesus Christ. That view is unteneble, however, because the cult of Lord

Krishna did not appear among the Hindus until after about 130 A.D.

Because the Apostle "Doubting" Thomas took the Gospel of Christ to India only a few years after the death of Jesus (his grave is known at Madras, India), it is obvious that the story of Jesus pre-dated the story of Krishna amongst the Hindus. Even though Hinduism is very much older than Christianity, it was the Hindus who stole the Christ concept and debased it into the cult of Krishna — not the other way around.

The Christ: Which One?

The word "christ" is an English transliteration of the Greek word *cristos*, which directly translates to "savior" or "messiah" (Hebrew). Christians identify Christ as Jesus who came in fulfillment of prophecy to save mankind.

New Agers differ from Christians regarding the concept of Christ. Whenever you hear New Agers, occultists or so-called "gnostic Christians" talking about "the Christ spirit," be aware that they are not using the term in any Christian sense. They will even talk about "Jesus the Christ" but only mean the mortal man Jesus who was temporarily posssessed by the Christ spirit.

The Christ Spirit is defined several ways in New Age literature: it is energy, a force and a principle among other things.[16] In regards to "the Christ" being energy, be aware that New Agers see occultism as the "hidden science of energy," not as black magic.

The "Christ as energy" viewpoint appeals to modern science for its validity, particularly the branch of physics called "quantum mechanics." This scientific discipline is the physicist's way of describing happenings on a subatomic level. Interestingly enough, quantum mechanics had led many physicists into Eastern religion and mysticism.

It appears that some findings of the scientists have close parallels in Zen Buddhism in particular. Some scientists are now claiming that matter seems to have consciousness, a concept of revolutionary consequence if it were true.

The "New Physics" relation to mysticism is expounded in books such as *The Tao of Physics* by Fritjof Capra, *The Dancing Wu Li Masters* by Gary Zukav and *Mysticism and the New Physics* by Michael Talbot.

Another book in this vein (but which argues from a different perspective) is *The Cosmic Code* by Eric Pagels, who is husband of Elaine Pagels (author of *The Gnostic Gospels*).[17]

New Age teaching also holds that the Christ is not an individual, either human or spiritual, but an office. The office passes from one being to another throughout history. According to Benjamin Creme in his book *The Reappearance of the Christ and the Masters of Wisdom*, the office of "Christ" has been held for the last 2,600 years by a being called Lord Maitreya.[17] He is said to periodically manifest himself in the flesh for the benefit of mankind. In addition to "His Disciple, Jesus," Lord Maitreya has appeared as Appolonius of Tyana, Mohammet, Krishna and others.

New Agers continually try to invoke Lord Maitreya through chanting the "Great Invocation" through constant repetition of the power number "666" and by other magical means. It was Lord Maitreya whom the theosophists tried to have possess Jiddu Krishnamurti in 1929. Certain New Agers claim that Lord Maitreya has been back in the world since the summer of 1977; he entered by airplane, they say.

The "Christ energy" that empowers the holder of the "Christ Office" is supposedly part of a cosmic consciousness, a god immanant in all things. All of the universe is said to be alive, that is, it's one immense living, conscious organism. The universal energies are focused into this world through the office of the christ.

The purpose of the Christ Energies is to educate earth inhabitants (and presumedly the earth itself, since it has consciousness) about their divinity. It (He?) is the "Supreme Educator," the principal driving force behind creation on the earth. As representative of the Hierarchy, Christ has the job of directing human development up the ladder of consciousness to eventual divinity. As our guide, the New Age Christ is our link to God — but bear in mind that Lucifer is supposed to be our link to Christ!

New Agers call Christ many things: "planetary power," "cosmic consciousness," "manifestation of the soul of the universe," "supreme education force" and the "basic evolutionary force." What they refuse to acknowledge, however, is that Jesus is the Christ, the one Christ and the only Christ — the Son of God. New Age doctrine collapses when the reality of the true Christ is acknowledged. For this reason alone the New Ager must invent an artificial Christ!

What The Scriptures Say

Between liberal Christians, New Agers and the claims of certain competing religions we have a variety of "Jesus figures" to choose from. But all of those sources lack a very important factor: first-hand knowledge of this man Jesus. All of them resort to either strained interpretations of scripture or to manuscripts that talk of someone else with a similar (and possibly fabricated) history.

They make the Essenes' Teacher of Righteousness or the Hindu's Saint Issa into a Jesus-like figure by the weight of sheer speculation — but speculation that is often as not taught as if it were the truth.

Such a ploy is, incidentally, called the "Argument

from the Stolen Concept," i.e., the making of something (or someone) into something they are not by replacement and frequent repetition. By replacing Jesus with the "Teacher of Righteousness" or "Saint Issa" or someone else, they eventually come to believe that Jesus was indeed someone else. It is critical for their beliefs that Jesus be almost anyone else except who he really is!

Given that other sources on the identity of Jesus are terribly flawed, what is a better source? Far superior are sources written by either eyewitnesses who knew Jesus personally or by people who associated with and were taught by the original eyewitnesses. There is a document in existence that was written by such people, we call it *The New Testament*. Springing to mind immediately is II Peter 1:16-19:

> "For we did not follow cleverly devised tales when we made know to you the power and coming of our Lord Jesus Christ but we were *eyewitnesses* of His majesty. For when He received honor and glory from God the Father, such an utterance as this was made to Him by the Majestic Glory, 'This is My beloved Son with whom I am well pleased,'— and **we ourselves heard this utterance made from Heaven** when we were with Him on the holy mountain" [NASB] [Emphasis added].

Concerning the identity of Jesus, the same eyewitness account tells us:

> "For God so loved the world that He gave **His only begotten Son**, that whoever believes in Him should not perish but have eternal life" (John 3:16 NASB) [emphasis added].

The witness in the Gospel of John is that God sent not merely His son but his "… only begotten son." Using the rule of document interpretation that admonishes "when the plain sense makes sense seek no other," we can only conclude that *Jesus was and is the Son of God and that there is no other.*

In Romans 1:2-4, the Apostle Paul likewise identifies Jesus. Paul writes to Roman believers:

> *"... concerning His son, who was born of a descendent of David according to the flesh, who was declared the Son of God ... "* [emphasis added].

Note in the above that Jesus was not called "a son of God" but rather, THE Son of God. The singular usage puts to shame the doctrine of the New Agers that we are all equally divine with Jesus.

In the Gospel of Matthew (16:13-17) Jesus asks Peter the basic question: " ... but who do you say that I am?" Simon Peter's answer tells the whole story: *"Thou art the Christ, the Son of the Living God."* Jesus concludes the conversation not by rebuking Simon Peter for error but rather by affirming the truth of his observation: "Blessed are you, Simon Barjona, because flesh and blood did not reveal this to you but my father who is in heaven."

Are the Bible Manuscripts Accurate?

The answer to the question of Jesus' true identity rests squarely on the Christian scriptures. The validity of the Christian viewpoint is directly related to the validity of scriptures. For this reason, liberal and New Age scholars have openly attacked the scriptures. Several of their questions must be confronted: when were the New Testament books written? How true are our modern transcripts to the originals? Did the Christian church alter the original manuscripts to eliminate valid doctrines?

The date of authorship of the New Testament becomes so controversial because key doctrines are affected. Liberal and conservative churchmen have opposite views of the Bible. The conservative believes that the scriptures are inerrant and are to be taken literally except where either metaphor or allegory is clearly intended by the writer; to the conservative the scriptures are both accurate and believable.

The liberal, on the other hand, believes that the scriptures are merely a doctrinal statement rather than an accurate historical account. Implicit in the liberal view is that Christian doctrine is relative and flexible — in other words, arbitrary.

The conservative sees doctrine as fixed by none other than God and is thus absolute for all time. The liberal diminishes the authority of scripture, while conservatives maintain the Reformation position that there is no other binding authority.

Because of their position regarding scripture, liberals must insist on late-dating New Testament authorship. Accordingly, liberals prefer a mid- to late-second century A.D. date for the authorship of the New Testament. Such dating would place 100 to 150 years between the actual events and the recording of those events, eliminating the authority of the eyewitnesses. Conservative opinion usually holds that the New Testament was written approximately mid-first century A.D. and was certainly completed with the writing of the *Book of Revelation* no later than 96 A.D.

The great time span represented by a second century dating is crucial to the liberals' view because of their claim of inaccuracies in the text. If the New Testament documents were written during the first century A.D., then errors and inaccuracies would be challenged by living eyewitnesses to the events recorded in the manuscripts. The "Eyewitness Effect" is a very powerful argument for the truth and accuracy of the New Testament — if it can be shown that the manuscripts were in circulation during the late first century period.

Conservative Christians believe that all New Testament books were written sometime prior to 96 A.D., with most of them being written in mid-century. This dating allows for scrutiny by eyewitnesses. A discussion of New Testament dating is presented in simple but elegant style by Josh McDowell in his book *More Than A Carpenter.*[18] McDowell appeals to several known manuscripts (MSS.): the Ryland MSS. (130 A.D.), the Beatty Papyri (155 A.D.) and the Bodmer Papyri II (200 A.D.) implying that these copies were based on earlier MSS.

Eminent authorities, some of whom previously adhered to the second-century position, now believe the entire New Testament was written between 40 A.D. and 90 A.D.; some of these men teach that all New Testament MSS. were completed and in circulation by the fall of Jerusalem in 70 A.D.

The research of Fr. José O'Callahan regarding the MSS. fragments found in Qumran Cave VII (which other scholars proved were sealed not later than 50 A.D.) is that they come from the Gospel of Mark. This finding is exciting to conservative Christians and absolutely devastating to liberal Christians' second-century contention.

The question of New Testament accuracy, apart from the issues relating to dating of the text, also involves the translation from oral tradition to written record. The claim is made that a great deal was lost or altered in transmission. Scholars who have studied oral histories tell us that such information can easily be transmitted with extreme accuracy, as witnessed by the consistency of primitive African tribesmen who memorize the oral history of their own people.

Accurate transmission was all the more likely in a first-century Jewish culture where pupils were used to sitting at the feet of their teacher, rabbis like Jesus, and memorizing their words (a practice that still exists in some orthodox Jewish communities). In such a culture textual losses over only one generation are considered negligible, especially when the older generation was still around to correct the record.

Although no record exists, it is also possible that some eyewitnesses to Christ's ministry on earth took notes or kept the equivalent of a diary. Literacy was widespread in Judaea because of the responsibility for men to read the scriptures in the synagogue and, according to one source "... the Greeks and the Jews were addicted to writing things down."

A second argument for the accuracy of transmission is (again) the Eyewitness Effect. Jesus' ministry was witnessed by thousands of Jews and gentiles and those many eyewitnesses served as a quality control factor over the written record that we now call the New Testament.

A third argument is to compare the *New Testament* with other ancient manuscripts over which there is little or no controversy regarding their accuracy to the originals. There are more than 20,000 existing New Testament manuscripts from the first several centuries of church history, some of which are dated only a few years after the events they describe.

By contrast, no other ancient document is so well supported. For example, Homer's *Iliad*, which ranks second only to the *New Testament* in number of surviving manuscripts, is supported by only 643 MSS. Other MSS. are even less well supported: the history of Thucydides is derived from only eight MSS. that date from 1300 years after the originals were written; the history of Herodotus, the works of Aristotle and Julius Caeser's *Gallic Wars* have even fewer copies in existence.

Why is it that scholars who would never think to

doubt the accuracy of Thucydides, Herodotus, Aristotle or Julius Caeser in their known editions almost automatically claim that the *New Testament* renditions are somehow defective? Perhaps it is because they shudder over the implications — eternal consequences — of their own teachings.

We must conclude that the *New Testament* records of the identity and person of Jesus are accurate and reliable, at least in their original form.

But what about the modern *New Testament*? Some people assert that the early church fathers excised certain doctrines and embarrassing details from the text of the New Testament. Two doctrines are favored for this claim: reincarnation and the identity of Jesus. Another claim is that the original Greek MSS. were accurate but are now lost and that all of the translations or later Greek copies are defective.

Two arguments come to bear against the assertion that the Bible was intentionally altered. First, the known early *New Testament* editions agree textually with the modern renditions. Second, the assertion falls rather quickly because it fails the test of reasonableness.

In order to support the view that the early church fathers altered scripture we would have to believe that they felt a pressing need to eliminate certain doctrines in favor of others. Regarding reincarnation vs. resurrection, for example, why would it matter to the church which of these two it taught *unless they had good reason to believe one was true and the other was false?* It is simply not reasonable to assume that the patristic fathers would arbitrarily choose from several "scriptural" doctrines.

The usual scenario offered for the altered Bible theory claims that an early church council made the changes in secret. The Councils of Nicea and Hippo are sometimes cited by proponents of the theory.

There are two problems with this claim.

First, no church council could have remained secret for long in the contentious early church period — there would always be dissenters, traitors or the indiscreet who would spread the secret abroad.

Second, the world at the time of the alleged alterations was awash with *New Testament* copies. If 20,000 of them survived to modern times, then there must have been many scores of thousands more in circulation at the time.

Any attempt, secret or otherwise, to remove key doctrines was doomed from the start. Such a vain attempt would have met massive resistance from all quarters — far too much resistance to allow a possibility of success.

Some critics like to point to the fact that the canon of scripture was not closed until the fourth century A.D. By that time, there were scores of books in existence to confuse believers. Some of them were scriptural, some were doctrinally sound Christian books but were not of scriptural rank and others were either heretic or derived from competing gnostic and other religions.

The councils which set the canon selected as "scriptural" only those books that met strict guidelines, including apostolic origin. Some utterly perfect Christian works were not accepted because they were not attributable to one of the original apostles or their near associates. Heretic books were rejected both on the grounds of non-apostolic origin and heresy. Those books cannot be regarded as "removed" from the Bible, as critics assert, because they were never in the Bible in the first place!

It is obvious to even the casual student that the

New Testament documents were written by eyewitnesses contemporary with other eyewitnesses to the actual events, are accurate records of the events and are (even in modern form) faithful to the originals.

Why Is the Question of Jesus' Identity So Important?

The quality of the New Testament record is important because it determines the identity and work of Jesus Christ. But why is the identity and work of Jesus so important? After all, wasn't he merely an outdated religious teacher who lived 2,000 years ago? The importance of these questions lies in the fact that salvation is at stake for all eternity.

In Christian belief, a soul is either reconciled to God through Jesus and gains eternal life or is damned to eternal punishment in the company of Satan and all his demons. Reconciliation with God is possible, according to those scriptures whose accuracy we have just established, only by accepting Jesus as Savior ("Christ", "Messiah" and "Savior" are synonims).

Christian doctrine stands in sharp contrast to all other religions. The Christian believes that salvation is through grace — unmerited divine favor — not works. All other religions teach some form of works are needed to earn salvation.

Christianity is almost unique in teaching that there is only one chance for the soul to gain salvation — there is no second chance either after death or in future lifetimes. So we come to a primary question regarding the prudence of your beliefs. If you died in the next minute, what would you tell God is the reason that He should let you into heaven?

Consider two views — the non-religious and the non-Christian religious — and then let's compare what will happen to both you and me if the other is right.

First, the non-religious.

If the non-religious person is correct and the Christian is incorrect, then both of us will become extinct at death and neither is worse off. But in the meantime, I have lived a life of hope and joy, while you lived a life of hopelessness " ... alone and afraid in a world you never made." *Which is most prudent?*

Also, if there is a second chance then the non-religious person is in no danger for he would surely choose God over damnation. Neither of us would be worse off than the other: one would gain salvation in the first chance and other in the second. But what if there is no second chance? Then the Christian is saved and the non-religious person is damned in hell; *which is most prudent?*

Now let's consider other religions or cults, neither of which accept the Christian belief regarding salvation. They claim either a different path to God or that all paths are equally valid for different people.

As our example, let's consider the position of the reincarnationist. If he is right and I am wrong, then my only penalty is another reincarnation or two, a mere 50 to 100 years out of my allotted millions of years. But if I am right and he is wrong, then I am saved while he is damned for not accepting Jesus during his one and only incarnation; *which position is the most prudent?*

As you should plainly see by now, there is very little hope for the non-Christian — and none of the non-Christian positions is prudent for the intelligent person. Although some people might denigrate "fire insurance" conversions, I suspect that God nonetheless rejoices at every decision for Christ.

References

And Chapter Notes

Chapter 1

1. Dave Hunt, *The Seduction of Christianity*, Harvest House (Eugene, OR, 1985).

2. See Constance Cumbey, *Hidden Dangers of the Rainbow*, Huntington House (Lafayette, LA) and *A Planned Deception: The Staging of a New Age Messiah*, Pointe Publishing Company. For a dissenting opinion, see Doug Groothius, *Unmasking the New Age*, InterVarsity Press.

3. See Joseph J. Carr, *The Twisted Cross*, Huntington House (Lafayette, LA).

4. Marilyn Ferguson, *The Aquarian Conspiracy*, J.P. Tarcher (Los Angeles, 1980).

Chapter 2

1. Shirley MacLaine, *Out On A Limb*

2. Shirley MacLaine, *Dancing In The Light*

3. Joseph J. Carr, *The Twisted Cross*, Huntington House (Lafayette, LA).

4. Compare several sources: James Webb, *The Occult Establishment*, Open Court Publishers (LaSalle, IL); Joseph J. Carr, op-cit; Harry Benjamin, *Everyone's Guide to Theosophy*, Theosophical Publishing House London, Ltd. (London, apparently not under copyright but preface dated 1969).

5. Many of the early church councils are sometimes cited as the perpetrator of the deed. In *Out On A Limb*, it was the Council of Constantinople in the sixth-century. The arguments against that selection are the same as for the Council of Nicea or others.

6. *The Lost Books of the Bible*

7. *The Book of Enoch*
8. *The Nag Hammadi Library in English*
9. Elaine Pagels, *The Gnostic Gospels*
10. Morton Smith, *The Secret Gospel*
11. G.R.S. Mead, "The Reincarnationists of Early Christendom," *The Quest*, April 1914; Reprinted in *A Quest Anthology*.
12. Ian Stevenson, *Twenty Cases Suggestive of Reincarnation*,
13. This list was developed in part from Mark Albrecht, *Reincarnation: A Christian Appraisal* and John Snyder, *Reincarnation Vs. Resurrection*
14. See the catalog for the exhibition, David Altshuler (editor), *The Precious Legacy, Judaic Treasures From the Czechoslovak State Collections*, Summit Books (New York, 1983).
15. Tal Brook, *The Other Side of Death*,

Chapter 3

1. See Dave Hunt, op-cit
2. See James Webb, *The Occult Establishment*, Open Court (LaSalle, IL) and *The Occult Underground*, Open Court (LaSalle, IL).
3. Ibid.
4. Josh MacDowell, *Handbook of Today's Religions*.
5. See *Webster's New Collegiate Dictionary*.
6. *How To Respond To The Occult*, Concordia Publishing House Series.
7. Ibid.
8. Ibid.
9. Ibid.
10. Definition developed from several sources: *Webster's New Collegiate Dictionary*; Dave Hunt, *The Seduction of Christianity* and several sources within the occult literature.

11. Rock music owes much to Aleister Crowley (see Jacob Aranza, *Backward Masking Unmasked,* Huntington House (Lafayette, LA). There are a number of sources on Crowley.

12. Ibid (Concordia Series book); see also (Weldon book)

13. See Shakti Gawain, *Creative Visualization;* Elissa McClain, *Rest From The Quest,* David Spangler, *The Laws of Manifestation.*

14. Elissa MacLain, *Rest From The Quest,* Huntington House (Lafayette, LA).

15. Raphael Gasson, *The Challenging Counterfeit.*

16. Ibid.

17. Merrill Unger, *The Haunting of Bishop Pike*

18. Ibid (Benjamin).

19. Ibid.

20. This person claimed that she is not a "medium" but rather a "channeler." This same term was used for the two mediums in *Out On A Limb.* Although some New Agers object to the terminology of spiritualism, the activity looks nonetheless like mediumship.

21. Ruth Montgomery, whose books popularized psychic seeress Jeane Dixon, made such claims.

22. It is sometimes necessary to make a composite definition in order to convey true meaning as used in the occult literature. It is not proper to simply "proof word" a topic without considering interrelated words and meanings.

23. Michael Harner, *The Way of the Shaman,* Harper & Row (New York, 1980); paperback edition published by the Bantam New Age Library 1982.

24. Ibid (Harner).

25. Ibid (Aranza).

26. Johanna Michaelson, *The Beautiful Side of Evil*
27. Ibid (Elissa McClain)
28. Joseph J. Carr, *The Twisted Cross*, Huntington House (Lafayette, LA).
29. Recommended reading: Kurt Koch, *Christian Counseling and Occultism*.

Chapter 4

1. This tradition [called variously "The Ancient Wisdom" and "The Ageless Wisdom"] was the basis of many European and Middle Eastern (basically gnostic) mystery religions. David Spangler, a leading New Age spiritual teacher, admitted that there is essentially nothing new in the New Age during a lecture series at The Association for Research and Enlightenment in Virginia Beach, VA.
2. Two of Bailey's books are especially anti-semitic. See *The Rays and the Initiation* and *Externalization of the Hierarcy*.
3. Norman Geisler, *False Gods of Our Time*, Harvest House (Eugene, OR, 1985).
4. Ibid (see both Geisler and Groothius).
5. Benjamin (op-cit); see also Robert Ellwood, *Theosophy: A Modern Expression of the Wisdom of the Ages*, Quest books (Wheaton, IL 1986).
6. Ibid.
7. Richard J. Foster, *Celebration of Discipline*, Harper & Row (San Francisco). Earlier printings of this book are especially revealing (see page 170).
8. Op-cit (Dave Hunt)
9. See Stephen Hoeller, *The Gnostic Jung*, Quest Books (Wheaton, IL).
10. Op-cit (Cumbey).
11. Op-cit.

12. Miller's article in *Moody Monthly*
13. For a description of two similar (but differing) views of Christian interpretation of prophecy see Hal Lindsey, *Late, Great Planet Earth* and Dave Hunt, *Peace, Prosperity and the Coming Holocaust.*
14. All of Schaeffer's books are available from Crossway Publishing: *The Complete Works of Francis Schaeffer.*
15. See Cumbey (op-cit) and also *The Findhorn Garden.*
16. Ibid (Foster).
17. See David Lewis' *Prophecy Intelligence Digest* (Springfield, MO).
18. Earl Paulk, *Satan Unmasked*, K-Dimension Publishers (Atlanta, GA).
19. Ibid (Paulk).
20. Meeting appears to have been sponsored by the Vienna Assembly of God church (Vienna, VA).
21. Ibid (Paulk).
22. Meeting held at Westpark Hotel, Tysons Corners, VA (near Washington, DC, October 16, 1986).
23. Constance Cumbey, *A Planned Deception*, Pointe Publishing.
24. Constance Cumbey, *Hidden Dangers of the Rainbow*, Huntington House (Lafayette, LA).
25. C. Matriciano, *Gods of the New Age*

Chapter 5

1. Rudolf Arnheim *(Visual Thinking);* Adelaide Bry *(Visualization: Directing the Movies of Your Mind);* Melita Denning and Osborne Phillips *(Creative Visualization for the Fulfilment of Your Desires);* Shakti Gawain *(Creative Visualization);* Dave Hunt *(The Seduction of Christianity);* Donald G. Matzat, "Is There A Seduction in Christianity Today?" *(Bread of Life Parts I-III).*

2. Marilyn Ferguson, *The Aquarian Conspiracy*, J.P. Tarcher (Los Angeles, 1980).

3. Richard J. Foster *(Celebration of Discipline)*; Dr. Norman Vincent Peale *(Dynamic Imaging)*; Rita Bennett *(Emotionally Free)*.

4. Dave Hunt, *The Seduction of Christianity*, Harvest House (Eugene, OR 1985).

5. Derived in part from several dictionaries and in part from Hunt (see above).

6. It is "words of power," a concept from occultism, that distinquishes sorcery incantations from prayer.

7. Leland R. Kaiser, Ph.D; "New Success Roles for Nursing Administrators." Photocopy used as seminar handout (original source unkown but appears to be a textbook).

8. Shakti Gawain, *Creative Visualization*, Whatever Publishing (Mill Valley, CA 1978).

9. Gavin and Yvonne Frost, *The Magic Power of Witchcraft*, Bantam New Age Books (New York, 1980).

10. Michael Harner, *The Way of the Shaman*, Bantam New Age Books paperback edition (New York, 1982). Also see *Hallucinogens and Shamanism* by the same author.

11. Ibid (Harner).

12. Confirmed by interviews with present and former visualization practicers, including Elissa McClain *(Rest From The Quest)*.

13. A.W. Tozer, *That Incredible Christian*, p.70

14. Tozer, p.69

15. Johanna Michaelson, *The Beautiful Side of Evil*, Harvest House (Eugene, OR 1982).

16. For more information on Silva Mind Control see *Larson's Book of Cults*, Bob Larson, Tyndale House (Wheaton, IL, 1982).

17. Rita Bennett (op cit)
18. Personal testimonies of visualizers.

Chapter 6

1. Stephan Hoeller, *The Gnostic Jung and the Seven Sermons to the Dead*, Theosophical Publishing House (Wheaton, IL, 1982). p. 387
2. Hoeller (op cit), p. xxi
3. Hoeller (op cit)
4. James Webb, *The Occult Establishment*, Open Court Press (LaSalle, IL, 1976), p. 347.
5. Ibid, p. 384
6. Ibid
7. Hoeller (op cit), p.3
8. Hoeller (op cit), p.4
9. Hoeller (op cit),p. 29
10. Hoeller (op cit), p.30
11. Hoeller (op cit),p.3 1
12. Hoeller (op cit),p. 7
13. Webb (op cit),p. 37 1
14. Ibid, p.38 1
15. Ibid.

Chapter 7

1. Personal experience
2. Modern term for what are essentially mystical or shamanistic practices; compare Harner (op-cit).
3. For a particularly interesting look at this phenomena see any of the Carlos Casteneda books, especially *Journey to Ixtlan.*
4. Carr (op-cit).
5. Webb, both books (op-cit).
6. See Webb (op-cit); and William James, *The Varieties of Religious Experience.*
7. Ibid (Webb).

8. Ibid.
9. Ibid.
10. Ibid.
11. Ibid.
12. Ibid.
13. Ibid (Webb). For additional information, read the works of the Beat authors, notably Ginsburg and Kerouac.
14. Ibid (Webb).
15. Ibid (Webb). See also Johanna Michaelson (op-cit).
16. Michaelson (op-cit); see also Rabi Maharaj, *Escape Into the Light*.
17. Michaelson (op-cit) and Maharaj (op-cit).
18. Simeon Edmunds, *The Psychic Power of Hypnosis*, see also Martin and Diedre Bobgan, *Hypnosis and the Christian*.
19. Ibid (Edmunds).
20. Ibid (Edmunds).
21. Ibid (Edmunds).
22. Ibid (Edmunds).
23. Ibid (Bobgans).

Chapter 8

1. See Constance Cumbey, *Hidden Dangers* ... (op-cit).
2. Ibid (Cumbey); see also David Spangler, *Reflections On The Christ*.
3. C.S. Lewis, *Mere Christianity*.
4. Ibid (Benjamin).
5. Ibid.
6. Spangler (op-cit).
7. (Benjamin) (op-cit)
8. The term seems to amuse Spangler but was created by the publisher of his book *Emergence: The Rebirth of the Sacred*.

9. Spangler, *Reflections* (op-cit)

10. H.P. Blavatsky, *The Theosophical Glossary.*

1 1. H.P. Blavatsky, *The Secret Doctrine.*

12. Alice Bailey, *The Destiny of the Nations.*

13. Albert Pike, *Morals and Dogma of the Ancient and Accepted Scottish Rite of Freemasonry.*

Chapter 9

1. Seth J. Farber, "The Crisis of Secular Authority: Modern Ecclesiastical Responses to the State," *The Humanist,* Jan/Feb 1983, pp. 13- 14.

2. John J. Dunphy, "A Religion For a New Age," *The Humanist,* Jan/Feb 1983, pp. 13- 14.

3. Benjamin Creme, *The Reappearance of the Christ and the Masters of Wisdom.*

4. Cumbey, *Hidden Dangers* ... (op-cit).

5. In fact, Spanger tells this initiation is Luciferic. See *Reflections on the Christ.*

6. Lucis Trust can usually be trusted to provide information on festival activities every year.

7. Lola Davis, *Toward A World Religion For the New Age.* Ibid.

8. Spangler, *Reflections* (op-cit)

9. David Spangler, *Revelation: Birth of a New Age.*

Chapter 10

1. See also Cumbey *Hidden Dangers* ... (op-cit), *A Planned Deception* (op-cit); Dave Hunt *Seduction* ... (op-cit) and *Peace, Prosperity* ... (op-cit).

2. *Gods of the New Age,* Jeremiah Films (see also Matriciano book of same title op-cit).

3. *Pathway To Paradise?,* three one-hour TV shows produced by Channel-38 TV, Chicago. See Christian Information Bureau address in back section of *Hunt Seduction* (op-cit) for information on VHS video tape availability.

4. See first chapter and introductions to this book.

Chapter 11

1. Tal Brooke, *The Other Side of Death*
2. Some liberals assert that "Jesus" is a composite of several different teachers.
3. Joseph J. Carr, *The Twisted Cross*, Huntington House, Inc. (Lafayette, LA, 1985).
4. Benjamin Creme, *The Reappearance of the Christ and the Masters of Wisdom*.
5. Joscelyn Godwin, *Mystery Religions in the Ancient World*, Harper & Row (New York, 198 1).
6. Morton Smith, *Jesus the Magician*, Harper & Row (New York, 198 1).
7. *The Secret Gospel*, The Dawn Horse Press (Clearlake, CA, 1973, 1982).
8. Luke 2:4 1-50
9. Hans Jonas, *The Gnostic Religion* and Charles Frances Potter, *The Lost Years of Jesus Revealed*.
10. Ibid
11. Yes Bookstore, Washington, DC
12. Robinson (op cit)
13. David Estrada and William White Jr., *The First New Testament*, Thomas Nelson.
14. Janet Bock, *The Jesus Mystery*, Aura Books (Los Angeles, 1980).
15. Ibid
16. Madame Helena Petrovna Blavatsky, *The Secret Doctrine and Isis Unveiled*. Madame Blavatsky was a founder of the original Theosophical Society.
17. Elaine Pagels, *The Gnostic Gospels*,
18. Creme (op cit)